MURDER
OF A CURLY-HAIRED BOY

Who really killed
Willie Starchfield?

SUSAN PHILLIPS

Table of Contents

INTRODUCTION

The photograph of a child's body portrayed in the tabloid *Daily Sketch* is properly dressed in a dark blue jersey and threadbare grey knickerbockers. Long, brown curly hair surrounds the waxen features of a deceased boy aged approximately five years. Underneath the photograph is a Police plea for witnesses to the child's whereabouts on Thursday 8th January 1914; there is also a £500 reward for information leading to the offender's apprehension for murder.

This image of the waxen features of a dead child is sent for publication in the *Daily Sketch* newspaper for public consumption; a common practice at the time. The official description of the boy reads "*age, about seven; complexion, fair; hair, light brown, long and curly; eyes, hazel; one tooth missing in front of lower jaw; dress, navy blue woollen jersey, two buttons on shoulder; dark grey tweed knickers, home-made; light grey tweed waistcoat, home-made; red, white, and blue striped flannel shirt; brown socks; brown button boots; white and blue lining around tops; black soft hat with black braid around the crown.*"

1

The moral barometer of the broadsheets does not permit a photograph of a dead child to be published; the transgression of child murder tapping into public fears of the 'Other;' a construct of abnormal practice. Requests for information in a murder case are not uncommon. The dead boy's photograph, snapped by a Police 'Flashman,' is accompanied by a request for information. It fires the imaginations of dozens of readers, some of whom visit newspaper offices in the hope of payment for information about the case.

As shocking as it seems, this close relationship between the Police and the Press benefits both parties. Media coverage assists the Police with obtaining information, and a newspaper sells more copies when the subject is sensationalised. In 1914, 'middle-of-the-road' members of the public, at the time generally men, obtain their news from the tabloids like the *Daily Mirror* or the *Daily Express*. The 1870 Education Act was initially formed to ensure that all children attended school, but had proved ineffective. Therefore in 1880 a further Education Act ensured that attendance was compulsory for children aged between five and ten years; but it was impossible to truly enforce this as many children worked and their parents relied upon their income.

At the beginning of the 20th century, with a national population of around 40,000,000, the generation of children affected by this Act, who can read, come of age. They require a newspaper that provides them with short, punchy articles, not lengthy diatribes. The popular tabloid suitable for mass circulation is born using concentrated language, in contrast to the 'boring' broadsheet *Times*. The tabloids focus upon crime, scandal, romance, and sport, instead of independent political thinking.

The class system dictates that the *Times* newspaper is read by the so-called 'thinking man' although it is not above vitriolic hyperbole in the case of news reporting. Those members of the 'hoi polloi' who can read devour the progeny of the 'penny dreadful' (the 'ha'penny dreadful'), with its salacious illustrations of items such as the murders of 'Jack the Ripper.' The Pure Literature Society calls for the banning of 'penny dreadfuls' on the grounds of moral righteousness and concerns that the material in them will debase the minds of those who read them.

The shifting politics of the late 19th century are controlled by the Press Barons. In tandem with a decrease in working hours comes the advent of evening newspapers to inform the public of unfolding events. The growth of the railways assists with newspaper distribution countrywide, as the

London dailies compete with regional newspapers. At the beginning of the new century, the press entertains as well as informs its readership. Jingoism enjoys more than a nodding acquaintance with the political upheaval before World War One.

Lord Rothermere owns the Daily Mirror and his rival Lord Northcliffe, previously Alfred Harmsworth, is the owner of the Daily Mail, a halfpenny morning paper. Their newsprint provides a condescending world view to its readers. Northcliffe supports British troops in the Second Boer War with nationalistic messages in his papers. In 1909 he hires Robert Blatchford, a Socialist and supporter of a British Empire, to write of the dangers of a coming German menace. These articles are designed to induce scepticism of Liberal moderate foreign policy. Northcliffe is a powerful force and propagandist who demands that his staff *"get me a murder a day."*

Now, with the imminent transition from peace to war underlying daily life in 1914, the alarmist fear of a potential German menace takes centre stage. There is a general distrust of foreigners due to commonly-held stereotypes focusing on racial prejudice, which take on a broader social meaning when linked to socio-economic disadvantage. Many Eastern European immigrants are viewed with fear and suspicion because they are suspected of pro-

German sympathies in the run up to the declaration of war. Their very presence is seen as encroaching upon the daily lives of the already underprivileged and over-stretched poor classes.

Following the published details of Willie's murder, the Police are inundated with statements from members of the public reporting foreign-looking men in company with a young boy. The hunt for Willie's killer, and a satisfactory closure to the case, is of paramount importance to the Police to reinforce public confidence in them. Twenty-six years earlier, the misogynistic murders of five women in and around the Whitechapel district, the so-called 'canonical five,' occur. Strenuous efforts are made to identify the killer, whose pseudonym is 'Jack the Ripper,' but by 1914 the murders remain unsolved.

At the time of those murders, the resulting public outcry leads to the resignation of the London Police Commissioner. That unsolved case remains in public consciousness. It hangs over the Police as a 'Sword of Damocles,' urging them to bring Willie's case to a satisfactory and swift closure.

CHAPTER ONE

The Funeral: Monday 19th January 1914

According to Roman Catholic tradition, the boy's body, encased in an open casket, has been kept overnight in the parlour of his home at 191 Hampstead Road, London. This vigil is attended by friends and family with the local priest leading the prayers. As the night blurs into a damp, grey morning, Agnes, the boy's mother, kisses his pallid forehead in a final farewell and cuts a lock of his hair as a keepsake. The lid of the coffin is screwed down. The coffin is moved onto the funeral bier by the undertakers. Inside the house, Emily Longstaff, the landlady who sent the boy on an errand from which he never returned, closes the curtains in the house as custom decrees.

Emily assists Agnes with adjusting her black bonnet before they alight one of the carriages waiting outside the house. Along the road all the neighbours' curtains remain closed as a communitarian mark of respect. The coffin is slid inside the waiting hearse with glass sides, its matched pair of black horses whinnying in the pale light, steam emanating from their nostrils. The horses have black covers on their backs and black ostrich feather plumes over their ears. The undertaker and his assistants remove their top hats. They walk at a measured pace preceding the hearse and accompanying carriages to the end of the road. They then take their seats in the hearse. Along the way, men stand erect as the cortege passes, removing their caps and bowing their heads in respect.

The funeral cortege wends its way through the crowded streets to its destination: St Mary's Roman Catholic Cemetery; a bleak location adjacent to Kensal Green Cemetery. The choice of cemetery reflects Agnes' Irish heritage. St Mary's twenty-nine-acre site, established in 1858, records 12,500 burials in the following eight years. These contain the remains of many Irish migrants who came to England during the Great Famine which emanated from a natural cause of potato blight. The cortege passes the Gothic-style lodge and comes to rest in front of the chapel. Behind the chapel a sarcophagus commemorates the Irishwoman Mary Anastasia Power, with kneeling angels supporting its four corners[1].

Inside the chapel the tiny coffin is placed in the centre aisle. A Funeral Mass is said. Agnes is bereft and her sobbing is ceaseless. She is physically supported by family members who prevent her from throwing herself onto the coffin at the graveside. On an overcast day, the boy's body is laid to rest in front of a crowd of approximately 4,000 people, as estimated in that evening's newspapers[2]. A Police cordon is in place to contain the crowd.

Watching the burial at a distance within the crowd is the boy's father, John. The last time he saw Agnes, his estranged wife, was at the Inquest into their son's death. Police officers wearing plain clothes discreetly mingle with the crowds eavesdropping on their conversations. The Senior Police Officer commissioned with investigating the boy's death is also in attendance, ostensibly paying his respects. In fact, his main motive is gaining a further perspective of the case by studying the behaviour of the mourners.

Once the coffin is committed to the earth, the crowd begins to disperse, encouraged to do so by a large Police presence. The boy's father silently slips away unnoticed and unacknowledged, the mawkish sentiments of some individuals in the crowd ringing in his ears.

CHAPTER TWO

The Crime Scene: London, 8th January, 1914, around 4pm

In death, the boy appears asleep. One hand and little legs encased in brown boots protrude from the space under the seat of the third-class carriage of the 4.14pm shuttle service between Chalk Farm and Broad Street.

The North London railway operates a fifteen-minute service from Broad Street to Chalk Farm. It calls at Shoreditch, Haggerston, Dalston Junction, Mildmay Park, Canonbury, Highbury and Islington, Caledonian Road and Barnsbury, and Maiden Lane. Approximately one in three trains extend from Chalk Farm over the London and North Western Railway to Willesden Junction (low level). They call at Loudon Road, Kilburn and Maida Vale, and Queens Park. Additional trains run during the morning and evening rush hour, including Saturday morning, and return traffic during the early afternoon. There is an additional interchange facility at Chalk Farm which links up the mainline platforms with some of the local services out of Euston[1].

This is the age of craftsmen, so teak from the Burma forests is used to build the carriages, even in third class. Ordinary third-class fares are between one shilling and one shilling and tuppence[2].

George Tillman, a young apprentice sent on an errand by his employer, bends down to tie his shoelace and in so doing looks under the seat of his third-class carriage. He sees the boy's body and is perturbed that a child would go to sleep in that position. Very confused by this turn of events, he decides to alert the Guard, but is unable to attract anyone's attention from within the separated compartment of the carriage. Tillman is unaware that since 1912 on all trains there is a communication cord outside the carriage by the cornice. The window must be pulled down and the communication cord pulled sharply which operates the train's brakes by opening a valve. This alerts the train driver as it activates a red flag indicating from which carriage the cord has been pulled[3].

Tillman, in a frightened state, is forced to wait in company with what he now perceives is a body of a boy, until the train pulls into Dalston station. He jumps down onto the platform from the carriage and attracts the attention of the Guard, Charles Pett, who is at the other end of the train. The Guard's compartment with its clerestory roof is a feature of the North London rolling stock. Meanwhile, the train continues to Shoreditch. Urgent telephone calls are made to Shoreditch station where a Porter named Edward Cook enters the carriage. Believing the boy to be asleep, he says *"Come on, Sonny."* Receiving no response, and only then realising that the boy is dead, he gently removes the boy's body from under the seat where it lies on its right side. He places the boy in the Stationmaster's office. The importance of securing the crime scene or of destroying potential evidence does not occur to him. The Police arrive and begin their initial investigations[4].

Dr Henry Edward Garrett, the divisional Police Surgeon arrives and initially examines the body *in situ* at 4.40pm. The body is fully dressed. The boy's soft hat falls off and is replaced upon his long, brown curly hair. There is no blood beneath the boy's fingertips. The hands and knees are covered in dirt, presumably from the floor of the railway carriage. Garrett discovers that a slight feeling of warmth remains between the thigh and the abdomen, indicating that extinction of life is recent. The clothing is dry, unsoiled, and not disarranged, apart from torn buttons at the neck of the boy's jersey. The exposed parts of the body are livid with a little dried blood on the edge of the lips. The narrow, livid line around the neck becomes prominent under Garrett's examination[5].

The weather that day is dull and mild with overcast skies that are darkening towards evening. There is evening fog at St James Park. Further intimate examination of the body needs more light so, under Garrett's stewardship, the Police remove the boy's body to the privacy of the local mortuary at Shoreditch. The machinery of the Metropolitan Police now rolls into action and Chief Inspector William Gough of 'D' division is appointed as the officer in the case[6].

CHAPTER THREE

The First Autopsy: 9th January 1914,
Shoreditch Mortuary around 5pm

> *"Those who have dissected or inspected many (bodies) have at least learnt to doubt; while others who are ignorant of anatomy and do not take the trouble to attend it are in no doubt at all."* (Giovanni Battista Morgagni (1682-1771)

The post of Police Surgeon was formally established in 1829 by the Metropolitan Police Act. Under bright lights in the clinical space of the mortuary, Dr Garrett proceeds to ascertain how the boy died. The smell in the mortuary is of thymol and carbolic acid. The glass jars of embalming fluids and other chemicals line up on the shelves like soldiers. The surgical instruments lie ready for his hand. Now, Garrett's role is that of an Ombudsman for the dead. Garrett makes a visual inspection of the whole body before he proceeds to make the first incision.

He lifts the child's chin and perceives the same narrow, livid line around the neck that he noted in his brief examination of the body yesterday. He cleans the skin, noting new bruises as he works. He works swiftly and precisely. He notes the presence of the residue of currant cake and suet in both the large and small intestines. Finally, he lays down his implements and leaves the body to be attended to by his mortuary assistant. His job is done. The body is now in the hands of the State.

He will later testify at the Inquest[1] that Willie dies due to strangulation by *"a cord like a fiddle string or window blind cord,"* and there were indications of a struggle. He further opines that asphyxiation of the neck caused death within no more than two or three minutes. *"It was the work of one person who maintained firm pressure of the head against a firm surface. The murderer sat on the seat whilst the child sat on the floor."*

The Second Autopsy: 10th January 1914, Shoreditch Mortuary

> *"Let the conversation cease, let the laughter flee, this is the place where Death delights to help the living." (Giovanni Battista Morgagni (1682-1771)*

Garrett's handiwork is overseen by Dr Bernard Spilsbury, the charismatic Surgeon[2]. Spilsbury arrives at the morgue and is greeted with due deference by the staff. His autopsy notes, plus Garrett's initial findings, will form the basis of the Inquest on 15th January at Shoreditch Coroner's Court in Boundary Street. The Court is a regular venue for inquests, falling under the remit of Shoreditch Borough Council whose motto is 'more light, more power.' Spilsbury's star is in the ascendant as a celebrity, and he is fêted by the great and the good. He is the first and only Honorary Home Office Pathologist, latterly to be described as the 'Father of Modern Forensic Science.' Prior to Spilsbury's notoriety as a celebrity Pathologist, bodies were examined by 'faceless' practitioners with little or no forensic expertise.

Spilsbury presents himself as a solver of the 'mystery' of death and is always immaculately turned out and charismatic in court. His evidence has become pivotal in murder cases. His gift to a Jury is simplifying the complex findings of autopsy and forensic medicine within a trial. He came to prominence for his findings in the 1910 Crippen trial, in which his forensic evidence convicts the perpetrator. His Knighthood is assured following the infamous 'Brides in the Bath' trial in 1915. During the trial he nearly drowns a nurse in the courtroom while demonstrating the murderer's technique[3].

Spilsbury examined the exhumed remains of Katharine Armstrong, the wife in the Armstrong murder case of 1922, which culminated in the hanging of her husband, the only Solicitor ever to be hanged. It will be commented upon at a later Trial in which Spilsbury gives evidence that *"Spilsbury's courtroom performance focused critical attention on the practices of pathology itself, which threatened to destabilise the status of forensic Pathology."* In 1924, in conjunction with Scotland Yard, he develops a 'murder bag' for use at crime scenes. This initially consists of a kit containing items such as gloves, evidence bags, a magnifying glass, and swabs. Later, the kit is adapted to keep pace with changing advances in forensics[4].

Spilsbury's hand-written report[5] states that the body is of a well-nourished boy aged five years and seven months. His height is forty-five inches. Spilsbury notes down the incisions of yesterday's post-mortem. The boy's right pupil is contracted.

The fingertips are livid and the fingernails are long and unbroken. The lips are slightly swollen and there are two abrasions inside the lower lip opposite the sharp edge of the left central incisor. The upper central and lower left central incisors are loose with a little blood on them. The lower right central incisor is missing. There is a recent bruise on the upper right side of the chest at the end of the first rib. Other bruises are by the right temple and in front of the right ear. Under depression, there is a neck haematoma. Furthermore, there are marks to the neck indicating the recent application of a narrow, constricting band. Associated with the line of constriction are superficial scratches at the root of the neck, indicating that the child had attempted to remove the ligature with his own hands.

Spilsbury also records that the stomach and small intestine contain food content, as previously detailed by Dr Garrett. Spilsbury's forensic conclusion, in line with Garrett's opinion, is that the boy died of strangulation by external violence using a ligature to the neck. He was *status lymphaticus* and was likely to die more quickly than a healthy boy of the same age when subject to shock. The boy's death occurs in around one to two minutes. Spilsbury concludes his post-mortem examination and now awaits the date of the Inquest, knowing that the body will be viewed *in situ* by the Inquest Jury.

CHAPTER FOUR

First day of the Inquest: 15th January 1914,
Shoreditch Coroner's Court

Witnesses:
Mr John Starchfield, the boy's father
Mrs Agnes Starchfield, the boy's mother
Mrs Emily Longstaff, Landlady
George Tillman, Apprentice
Edward Joseph Cook, Porter
Charles Pitt, a Railway Guard
*Chief Inspector William Gough, Officer in Charge of
the case*

Today, the Inquest into the cause of Willie's death
will be opened by Dr Wynn Westcott, the Coroner,
who has been appointed to sift the evidence in the
case[1]. The roots of the Inquest process originate
with the Articles of Assize, which empower the
Coroner to act for the Crown in a peripatetic
manner. Historically, from 1487 a Coroner is
reimbursed one mark per inquest in the case of a
murder inquiry, plus a forfeit of fourpence from the
goods and chattels of the guilty person. The first
Coroners' Act of 1751 allocates twenty shillings per

case to each Coroner and provides a travel expense of nine pence per mile. These fees require authorisation by the local Justices of the Peace. A part of the Justices' remit is the financial control of the Coroners, which causes dissension between both parties and results in the restriction of Inquests into violent deaths. A further Coroners' Act is introduced in 1887 and standardises a Coroner's duties; which is primarily to investigate deaths.

In 1881, Westcott is appointed Deputy Coroner for Central Middlesex and Central London, and in May 1894 he becomes Coroner for North East London. Westcott is an active and enthusiastic Freemason who allegedly prefers ceremonies over banqueting. Westcott is also a renowned Necromancer, of whom Aleister Crowley, the English occultist, waspishly decrees *"Westcott was paid to sit on corpses, not to raise them.*[2]*"* In 1887, Westcott co-founds the Hermetic Order of the Golden Dawn with Samuel Liddell MacGregor Mathers and William Robert Woodman. This is a secret society devoted to the study and practice of the occult, metaphysics, and paranormal activities. During the late 18th and early 19th centuries mediumship and spiritualism has gained ground with the middle classes and some practitioners achieve cult status.

Westcott resigns from the Golden Dawn around 1896/97, following expressed concerns by his employers; ending his association with the Society due to its incompatibility with his post as Coroner.

Today, Westcott becomes the interface between the law and medicine in the proceedings of Willie's death[3]. Twelve 'good men and true' have been sworn in as the Jury. These be-hatted, mainly moustachioed men attend Shoreditch mortuary under Police guard to view the boy's body for themselves prior to the Inquest. In the week preceding the opening of the first day of the Inquest, the Police are inundated with reports from the public who have viewed the photograph of the dead boy in the newspaper. Some of the expressed interest is prurient, some solicitous.

Prior to the commencement of day one of the Inquest, several members of the public come forward in response to the appeals for information about Willie's whereabouts on the day his body is found. They are taken to the mortuary by the Police to view Willie's body. George Seabrook, 38 years, of number 1 Alma Street, Kentish Town attends at 2.30pm and identifies the body. In his witness statement, dated 11th January, he says he saw a lad resembling the photograph he saw in the newspapers. *"This lad was with a man, apparently a foreigner, aged between 28 and 36 years, 5' 4" in height. He had a dark complexion and rather conspicuous eyebrows. The man wore a light-coloured mackintosh or coat and a black bowler. His arm was around the lad who was carrying a small parcel under his arm. They boarded a tram from Euston to Hampstead.[4]"*

Another account is submitted by a Conductor employed by the Hampstead and Charing Cross Tube Railway. He states that on the afternoon of the murder, a man carrying over his shoulder a child answering the description of Willie is seen at Goodge Street Station, near Hampstead Road. The man alights at Camden Town Station. Furthermore, both the Driver and the Conductor of a motor omnibus tell the Police that they believe they saw the boy in company with a man of foreign appearance soon after 3pm on the day of the crime. The pair alight at Kentish Town rail station and disembark at Tuffnell Park tube station. The man with the boy is described as wearing a dark grey suit and seems out of temper with the child, who appears unwilling to go with him[5].

All these reports are carefully recorded on headed Metropolitan Police lined notepads, signed by the Duty Inspector, and co-signed as read by Chief Inspector William Gough of D Division[6]. Gough took charge as the Senior Investigating Officer in the case in the hours following the discovery of Willie's body.

Gough is also in possession of a cord that has been found on the railway line by a Signalman, which will be referenced in evidence. Gough is a main protagonist attending each day of the Inquest, keen to make an early arrest, and maintain his reputation as a 'thief-taker, and law enforcer.'

Now, Agnes Starchfield enters the courtroom. She is flanked by Police officers carrying umbrellas to potentially shield her from the estimated 300 strong crowd of sightseers outside. Agnes is dressed in stark black with a large black plume in her hat and is heavily veiled. John, her estranged husband, follows several paces behind her. Walter Sickert, an eccentric artist, is an attendee at the inquest[7]. Sickert inhabits a studio between 1910 and 1914 which is situated in Hampstead Road, not far from Agnes' abode. Sickert attends Willie's Inquest as an observer of social history. This stance allows him to insert himself into the Inquest in the position of 'eavesdropper;' observing the scene in the pursuit of his art. As a dispassionate observer, he swiftly sketches a likeness of Agnes when she removes her mourning veil to give her evidence. This 'on-the-spot' sketch shows a pretty, dark-haired woman with large eyes. His sketches underlie his recurring theme of recording the lives of the working classes.

Prior to World War One, Sickert's artistic populist appeal is limited in Britain because his pastels work is linked to the coolness of Degas' impressionism. This is compounded by his association with ultra-sophistication in the art world, and his frequent absences to Dieppe. The advent of the Camden Town Group of Post-Impressionist artists in 1911, with its core values of realism, recognise Sickert as a 'Master' of originality. This accolade is based upon his depictions of mundane life in the communal pastimes of the residents of North London. Although his critics condemn his work as 'sordid,' it is also recognised as an accurate portrayal of contemporary life at the time.

Sickert's interest in crime and the macabre is evidenced by his paintings known as the Camden Town Murder series. These are painted from the viewpoint of the 'male gaze' in the wake of the local murder of Emily Dimmock, a 23-year-old part-time prostitute. In this series of portraits there are several scenes depicting a fully-clothed man observing a naked woman lying on an iron bedstead. Sickert's narrative in this series of paintings is the female nude lying on a bed in a dingy interior environment.

Dimmock's murder, and the eventual murder Trial in which one of her lovers is found not guilty, garners much public interest being covered by the newspapers in minute detail. It conjures up a frightening reminiscence for the public of the unsolved Whitechapel murders twenty years before[8].

Westcott now enters the courtroom by another door. He is flanked by Basil Thomson, the Police Assistant Commissioner, who sits to the right of Westcott but does not speak. Thomson has spent the previous week in the company of Gough visiting the crime scene and keeping abreast of developments. His presence at the Inquest is a visual reminder to the participants that the Police are actively seeking a solution to the case. Westcott commences proceedings by expressing his condolences to both parents. He explains that his reason for delaying the Inquest by one week was in the hope that the case will have been completed at the end of today. Unfortunately, he is unable to produce any more information, or conclusive proof as to how the child died, so the Inquest must continue. Westcott comments on the amount of publicity that the case has engendered from the newspapers and expands upon the advantages and disadvantages of such publicity.

Westcott's spoken view is that *"while it might encourage people to hunt for the missing man, it tended to create a panic among parents who were not always able to keep their children under their eyes."* He turns to the Jury and reminds them that London *"has a lower rate of murder than any other capital in*

Europe," and remarks that the Jury will have to decide whether *"the murder may have been committed by either a homicidal maniac or a common criminal.*[9]*"*

A composed John Starchfield takes the stand, leaning heavily on a walking stick. His evidence is that he and his wife are separated and that he allows her £1 a week while they are separated. This money is obtained from his Carnegie Fund award for catching the murderer in the well-publicised Titus case in 1912. John states that he did not get up until 3.30pm on the day of the murder. He says that he felt unwell due to the wound he acquired in the Titus case. He had just returned from a public house on the day of Willie's death and had not gone to bed yet when the Police inform him of the murder at his lodgings at 12.30am.

Westcott asks *"Can you produce anyone who can prove that you stayed in the lodging-house until half past three on the day of the boy's death?"*

John replies that he can and he furnishes the Coroner with a man's name. He is prepared to swear that he did not see the boy that day and that he did not send anyone up to see his wife or the boy. He says that he last saw Willie approximately three weeks ago. After a few more general questions about John's movements on the day in question,

Westcott tells John to *"sit over there and we will ask you questions at our discretion."*

Agnes Starchfield begins to give her evidence. She is visibly distressed but insists on continuing. She confirms her address and marital status. She adds that her surname is actually Sarchfield, but her husband insists upon adding a 't' to it; an idiosyncrasy which belies the information written on her marriage certificate. She explains that Willie is her third child, her previous two children having died before the age of five. On the day of the murder, having been unable to find work, she went out at 11am to visit a friend. She leaves Willie in the care of Mrs Emily Longstaff, the landlady of her lodgings; a not unusual occurrence. On returning home around 3pm neither Willie nor Emily Longstaff is there. Emily returns some minutes later and informs Agnes that Willie is missing. Agnes relates how Emily sent Willie on an errand from which he did not return.

Westcott asks *"Can you account in any way for the boy's disappearance?"*

Agnes answers in the negative.

Westcott continues *"Has anyone ever taken him out for walks?"*

Agnes replies *"No Sir, except people in the house, and I always knew where he was going."*

Westcott considers this response then asks *"He never told you that anyone had taken him away?"*

"Once" the Witness replies, *"His father had sent him to the 'Pictures' alone, and another time a little boy took him to the 'Pictures'."*

Agnes says that she is convinced that this same boy did not take Willie away on the day of the murder. She then adds that Willie was fonder of her than his father and did not want to live with him. This statement gives an overt message to the Jury that Willie would not have gone willingly with his father on the day he died, if at all.

In reply to a question from the Jury Foreman, Agnes says that during her search for her son, she did not go her husband at his *Evening News* vending pitch situated opposite the Horseshoe Hotel in the Tottenham Court Road. At that stage she says that she did not want him to know that the boy was lost. She describes the circumstances in which she hears that Willie has not returned. She and Emily search for Willie in the local area with no success, visiting the newsagent's shop which is the last confirmed sighting of him.

Agnes explains that she suggests to Emily that they search toward Camden Town, the opposite way to the previous search, enquiring of the boy's whereabouts as they go.

The Coroner questions Emily closely, *"Had you any suspicion why the boy had not returned?"*

"None, whatever, Sir."

"There was no-one in the house who had any animosity against him or the mother?"

"No, Sir."

"Was she a quarrelsome person?"

"No, she never quarrelled with anybody."

"She lived a moral life with you?"

"Yes, Sir."

"Had she any men visitors?"

"No. Her brother came once."

Emily cannot remember whether she gave Willie chocolate that morning. She remembers that she had certainly not given him a meal. A member of the Jury asks if there were any lodgers employed on the North London Railway in the house. Emily replies in the negative.

The Juryman asks *"you do not know whether the child knew any railway servants?"*

"No, Sir."

Next on the stand is George Tillman, an apprentice, who unwittingly entered the same carriage as the dead child. He relates his business on the railway, his discovery of Willie's body, and how he attempts to alert railway staff. He only remembers two other passengers on the platform when he embarks at Haggerston Station.

Westcott asks *"did you touch the body?"*

"No, Sir. I watched to see if it moved. At that time, I thought possibly that the boy might be asleep. At the same time, I thought it strange that the child should be asleep under the seat. I continued to watch if it moved."

"Were you afraid of it?"

"Fright, Sir."

"When you entered that carriage at Mildmay Park did anyone get out of it?"

"No, Sir."

"Then you saw nothing to indicate how the body got there?"

"No, Sir."

Tillman relates how he alights at the next station, manages to alert a Porter of the boy lying under the seat, and then gives his name and address to the Station Master. Westcott thanks him for his evidence and calls Edward Joseph Cook to the stand. Cook identifies himself as the Porter who removes the boy's body from the train.

Cook relates how when he saw the child on the floor of the carriage, he believes that the child is asleep. He says *"Come on, Sonny."* Upon receiving no reply, he lifts the boy up and onto the platform. The child appears dead. Its legs and arms are cold. Cook says that there are no signs of a struggle in the carriage and he does not notice whether the windows were open. The floor of the carriage appears dry. In reply to the Jury Foreman, Cook says that the carriage is a non-smoking one.

Guard Pitt, in charge of the train, gives evidence that the carriages were swept out and examined at Broad Street. He himself looked through them twice during the afternoon before the train left Chalk Farm at 4.14pm for Broad Street. He took charge of the train shortly after 2pm and saw no-one carrying a parcel enter the train, nor did he notice the boy. There were very few passengers on that journey.

Westcott asks *"Did you see anyone carrying a child in their arms as if it were an invalid?"*

Pitt replies, *"No, I did not. If I had, it would surely have attracted my attention."*

Westcott directs his next remark to Chief Inspector Gough, commenting that the only thing that he would like to know now is whether a half ticket was sold that afternoon. Gough explains that every enquiry had been made about such a ticket, but no light can be thrown upon the matter. Gough recounts how *"diligent enquiries have been made in all possible directions."*

Gough continues *"Ticket collectors and others along the line were immediately seen and all the useful information which could be ascertained has been placed before the court. Enquiries were also made of employees at the Tube railways as well as servants employed on Hackney carriages, etc. to try and trace the movements of the boy after he was missed. Other enquiries were made to ascertain if he were seen at shops where cakes, etc were sold, but nothing of a tangible nature has resulted therefrom.*

With regard to the issue of tickets on the North London Railway, I find that a record is only kept for the purpose of finance and that after collection they are forwarded to Audit Office, Euston Station, and subsequently destroyed. Therefore, it is impossible to gain any useful information which might help to identify the parties purchasing them. The ticket collectors who were on duty on the 8th January attended the first hearing of this inquest but neither of them has been able to assist in the matter.

The movements of persons upon whom suspicion might have attached have been enquired into, but no evidence to connect anyone with the crime has been obtained to warrant any criminal notion. A great number of letters have been received by the police purporting to give information on the matter, but upon enquires it has been found that the writers were unable to advance the case. Although in many instances the informants were invited to attend the court, no good purpose was served.[10]"

Westcott now suspends the Inquest proceedings to re-convene on Thursday 22nd January so that Willie can be buried on 19th January at Kendal Rise Catholic Cemetery.

Second Day of the Inquest: 22nd January 1914, Shoreditch Coroner's Court

Exhibits Produced:

Four photographs of Willie's body: two naked and two clothed
The clothing of the deceased child
A cake from Reiffs Bakery, Kentish Town Road

Witnesses:

Dr Garrett, a Divisional Police Surgeon
Dr Bernard Spilsbury, a Pathologist whose public prominence and use of everyday language at the Inquest enhances the public interest in the case
Joseph Rogers, a Railway Signalman
Jules Labarbe, a Frenchman, Manager of John Starchfield's lodging house
William Tilley, also known as William 'Barry', a street Vendor and resident of the lodging house, known to John Starchfield
Joseph Payne, also resident at the lodging house, and known to John Starchfield
Thomas Stickney, a Hotel Porter, and another lodger known to John Starchfield
James Lane, a Newsvendor
George Jackson, a Railway Signalman
William Morcher, an Engine Driver
John Starchfield, the boy's father
Mrs Clara Frances Ann Wood, wife of a Shop Blind Maker

Westcott, with due solemnity, resumes the Inquest proceedings. Agnes Starchfield is in attendance, but not as a witness. She buried her son three days ago, and is still in mourning dress. Today, the evidence is hard for her to hear, and she is supported by friends.

Dr Garrett is called to the stand. With the assistance of the photographs of Willie's body he describes the injuries that occurred, especially the marks to the neck. He states that there were all the signs of strangulation and some indications of a struggle. In answer to a question from the Jury Foreman, Garrett opines that the child was kneeling when the crime was committed. He comments that if a woman committed the crime, she could have placed the boy between her knees, provided she wore a loose skirt. A woman wearing a 'hobble' skirt would find the that the garment would interfere with such a movement, unless it were lifted.

'Hobble' skirts were briefly fashionable but by 1914 have declined in popularity due to the limited mobility that impedes the wearer. Garrett's initial examination shows signs of pressure on the abdomen, and his belief is that the child was held between the person's knees whilst the crime was committed.

Garrett explains that scratches and marks around the neck show a struggle in which Willie endeavours to remove the constriction around his neck with his own hands. The groove around Willie's neck indicates a narrow constricting band which may indicate the use of a blind-cord, a window-cord, or a fiddle string. Associated with this line of constriction are many superficial scratches at the root of the neck in front, extending over the breast bone. There is also an external bruise over a rib on the right side. The stomach contents contain an ounce and a half of partially digested food. Strangulation by external violence is the cause of death; Garrett's opinion is that death occurred between 2pm and 3pm on the afternoon of January 8th.

In response to a question by Westcott, Garrett's opinion is that there is no sign of an anaesthetic having been used. He calmly states that the boy had not been interfered with before being strangled[1].

Dr Bernard Spilsbury confirms Garrett's findings. Spilsbury reiterates from his own hand-written autopsy notes that Willie was *status lymphaticus* and therefore more likely to die more easily than an ordinarily healthy boy, if subject to sudden shock.

Westcott asks *"That would not mean that the boy would die that day?"*

"No. It would show danger of sudden death as the result of certain shocks."

"He would die more easily than a healthy boy if he were submitted to a sudden shock?"

"Yes, he would."

In Spilsbury's view this medical condition accelerates Willie's death within one minute of the tight application of a cord or a ligature surrounding the boy's neck. Spilsbury now refers to the finding of a piece of string by a signalman on the North London Railway Line between Shoreditch and Broad Street stations. This was found the day after the crime was committed. He indicates that this could have caused the boy's death. He adds that around one of the boy's arms was a mark similar to that of the mark around the neck. This suggests to him that the arm had been caught in the ligature around the neck and was removed before the ligature was finally tied. There are signs that the head was pressed against a hard surface, and there is evidence of firm pressure on the mouth. Spilsbury attributes death to asphyxia caused by strangulation, followed by heart-failure due to the previously mentioned *status lymphaticus*[2].

Spilsbury steps down from the witness box and is replaced by Joseph Rogers. He corroborates that he picked up a piece of cord which was lying near the Number 2 'up home' signal near the wall. He says he later passed his find to an Inspector. The cord found by Rogers is shown to Spilsbury who says that it could have caused the marks on Willie's body. The knot in the cord might produce such a bruise as he found on the back of the neck when examining the body[3].

Acknowledging Agnes' presence, Westcott states that the account of her movements on the day has been corroborated by friends upon whom she called, and from places where she sought work. He does not wish to cause her any more pain by calling her as a witness.

Turning to the Jury, he states that evidence will be called with reference to John's account of his whereabouts that day.

Jules Labarbe swears that he saw John in the lodging house on the morning of January 8th. Labarbe went out and returned at a quarter to two but did not see John on the premises at that time.

Westcott asks *"You say you looked in his bedroom?"*

"I am not sure. I think I may have."

"You won't swear that you looked in his bedroom and all over the house as usual?"

"No, Sir."

"You cannot swear that Starchfield and his friend were at home when you came back to the lodging house after going out?"

"No, Sir."

"Did you see him go out that day?"

"I cannot swear to it."

"Did you see him go out in the evening?"

"I cannot swear to that."

Westcott says *"it is rather curious that you told the police this, and now you deny it. You said Starchfield had been ill lately and had remained in bed longer than he might have done?"*

"Yes."

"Did you say that he had never been in bed after 1pm in the day except on Sundays?"

"I have said that."

"Will you say it again now?"

"No, Sir."

Westcott turns to the Jury and indicates Labarbe's statement, saying, *"Yet he says at the bottom of this paper: This statement has been read over to me, and it is true."*

"I do not know what reliance you can place on this evidence. It is very painful to suggest that the

father of the dead child had anything to do with it, but at the same time it is our duty to make sure that he did not."

In reply to the Foreman, the witness said that the beds were made at 10am by a servant. He saw John in bed on that particular day, at that time.

"People can get in and out of their bedrooms all day and all night?"

"Yes; up the other staircase."

"Then it comes to this: you will not swear he was on your premises after half past twelve?"

"No, Sir."

Tilley is next to give evidence. He explains that he sleeps in the same room as John. He told police that he left John in bed when he got up on 8th January. He says John was in bed at 8.30am.

Westcott asks *"You have sworn that he was in bed until 2.30pm?"*

"Yes. I didn't leave the house until nearly 3pm, and he had not come down then."

"You mean that you had not seen him come down?"

"Yes."

"You told the police you got up at 10 o'clock."

"I went out and I didn't return until 11.30 at night."

"Now you say you didn't go out until 2.30pm?"

"I didn't specify any time at all. He (the Police Officer) called me up at 3.30 in the morning when I was in a flurry, and I didn't know what I was saying. I was half-awake and half-asleep, and I didn't know what I was wanted for."

In answer to a question from the Jury Foreman, Tilley says he has known John for thirteen years and believed him to be fond of the boy[4].

Joseph Payne gives his evidence. He states that he saw John alone in the bedroom at 11.45am.

Westcott asks *"Then Tilley was not in bed? He swears he was in bed up to half past 2."*

"I don't remember seeing him there."

Thomas Stickney corroborates John's account and says he saw him dressing on the day of the murder at 2.50 pm.

James Lane, a Newsvendor, describes seeing John at 4.20pm in High Street, Bloomsbury[5].

Westcott calls George Jackson to the stand. He says that he is employed by the North London Railway at the St Pancras box. He declares that as the 2.14pm train from Chalk Farm to Broad Street passes at 2.18pm on 8th January, he is standing at the open window of his box and has a clear view of the train.

Jackson looks at the third-class compartment which is towards the front of the train. He sees a man with his face towards the engine leaning over someone whom he took at the time to be female. It was either a boy or a girl and the hair appears to be curly. The head is moving slowly. He sees only the side of the man's face, noting that he has a dark moustache, and is wearing a dark bowler hat and a dark coat.

Westcott muses *"it is not a very definite piece of evidence. It might not apply in this case, and on the other hand, it might."*

Jackson adds that when he attended the mortuary to view the child's body, he recognised Willie's face as that of the child in the carriage. He says that when standing in the box that he is only twenty-five feet from the train.

He relates *"My curiosity was aroused by seeing someone get up from the seat, and seeing the head and shoulders go back into the opposite corner. Then I saw the head more, and by that time the face was as low as the level of the woodwork of the window. Then the train was gone. It took about ten seconds. I spent most of my time looking at the face that I now know to be William Starchfield. Seeing the curls, I was under the impression that it was female."*

In reply to the Jury Foreman, the witness said that he could not identify the man as he only got a flash of him; but he must have been over twenty-five years of age[5].

Train Driver Morcher says that while engaged in shunting at the Camden coal yard, adjoining Chalk Farm Station, between 2.30pm and 3pm he saw a man in the third-class carriage of the train standing in the bay. The man was stooping as if he was tying up a parcel. He was a powerfully-built man with broad shoulders. He saw him again later in the same compartment still stooping. The compartment was the fourth in the second coach facing Broad Street. According to a colleague, the body was found in the last compartment but one of the second coach from the end.

Westcott says *"That is rather important."*

John is then recalled to the witness box. He denies going to Kentish Town or Camden Town on the day of the murder.

Westcott asks *"You did not take the boy anywhere that day?"*

John replies *"I never saw him."*

"You did not go on the North London Railway that day?"

"No, Sir."

Mrs Wood now gives her evidence[6]. She states that at 1.15pm on 8th January she was outside Messrs. Daniel's drapery shop when she saw a man and a boy walking towards her from the direction of Camden Town Station. The man was around 5'3" in height and about thirty-eight years of age. His complexion and hair were dark and he had a dark moustache. He wore a soft, felt hat. The boy was about five years old with thick brown curly hair and a round face. She could not describe his clothing in detail other than he wore a tight-fitting upper garment.

The man was holding the boy's right hand in his left hand. The child was munching on what appeared to be a piece of cake. Mrs Wood remembers commenting *"Oh, bless it,"* as they walked past as she is very fond of children and was pleased to see the boy enjoying his food. Furthermore, she has since been shown a photograph of Willie and says that he is the boy that she saw on that day.

Westcott hands her a photograph and asks if she recognises the person in it. She responds *"Yes, I do recognise him as the little boy."* She adds that the man was an 'Italian-looking man'. She relates how on January 17th she was passing Reiff's, a baker's shop in Camden, when she recognised the cakes in the window as similar to the one that the boy was eating.

At this point in the proceedings a child's jersey is handed to her and she says *"It is just like it. That is just how it fitted him."*

The Jury Foreman asks *"Have you seen the man again?"*

"Yes."

Where? "Here."

"Here?" repeats the Foreman, *"Where?"*

Mrs Wood looks round the room and for some moments she remains silent. Suddenly, her eyes rest upon John who is sitting close to his wife in the witness's row.

She points her finger and exclaims *"That is the man, sitting close to that lady."*

At this point Agnes bursts into tears and sobs violently.

She moans *"Oh, don't say that, don't say that."*

John springs to his feet and cries out *"Me?"*

Mrs Wood calmly says *"It is you. I am sorry, but it is you. This is the second time I have seen you today."*

"Me, leddy?" asks John.

"Yes" she replies.

John shouts *"It is a lie."* He then sits down.

Mrs Wood declares *"The moment I saw him I knew him. I saw him outside the court this afternoon."*

This dialogue causes great consternation among those present. Westcott and Chief Inspector Gough engage in muted conversation. The result of that conversation is that Westcott believes that it is eminently desirable and fair that a further opportunity should be given to the public, and to other persons, to call to mind matters which may lead still further to the identification of the father. This will assist in confirming or removing any suspicion that now lies on him. Agnes, in response to Westcott, states that she saw her husband wearing a cap on the day of the murder. She has never seen him wear a soft, felt hat.

Westcott adjourns the Inquest until the 29th January. John leaves the Inquest unhindered and walks off unnoticed by the crowd gathered outside.

Third Day of the Inquest: 29th January 1914, Shoreditch Coroner's Court

Witnesses:
Dr Bernard Spilsbury, a Pathologist whose public prominence and use of everyday language at the Inquest enhances the public interest in the case
Michael Ryan, Day Deputy at the lodging house
William Tilley, a street Vendor and resident at the lodging house
Mr Richard John White, a Commercial Traveller
Chief Inspector Gough, Police Officer in the case

In attendance:
Mrs Agnes Starchfield
Mr John Starchfield

Today, the Inquest evidence occupies just under two hours[1]. Dr Spilsbury reiterates his report of an analysis of the stomach contents of the murdered boy. Westcott says that this report has an important bearing on the evidence of Mrs Wood. Namely, that the boy was eating what appeared to be a piece of cake not long before his death. Dr Spilsbury says he has had cakes examined which were bought at the shop referred to by Mrs Wood in her previous evidence; he found small nut-like morsels in them. This type of cake might likely have formed the source of food of which he found traces in his examination of Willie's body.

Michael Ryan takes the stand and states that the police took a statement from him on the night of the murder. Westcott reads out the statement which records that Ryan saw John in bed at noon on the day of the murder. In the same room was Tilley[2].

Tilley, when recalled to the stand, retells the contents of his police statement, in which he maintains that he saw John in bed at 2.30pm. He adds that John did not leave the lodging-house until 3pm. This is in direct conflict with Agnes' statement on cross-examination. She maintains she saw Tilley in Rupert Street between 1230pm and 1245pm on that day[3].

A commercial traveller named John White next gives evidence. He describes seeing a man with a little boy standing together at Camden Town Railway Station on the 8th January. When asked to describe the man, Mr White is asked if he can point him out in court. White indicates John who is sitting in one of the seats reserved for witnesses saying

"That is the gentleman."

John at once springs up and protests in a loud voice "It is a lie."

Tilley, in support of John's alibi, vocally joins in the denial.

White states that he heard the man whom he saw at the station calling the boy. The Jury Foreman asks if he recognises the voice.

He responds *"Yes, I know the man; I will swear to it."*

White's evidence[4] is that on 8th January shortly before 2pm he was in Camden Town Station. A man holding a little boy by the hand entered at the Kentish Town entrance. He describes the man as having an 'Italian-like' appearance and wearing a dark overcoat and hat. He says the boy is of dark complexion and slim build. The man leaves the boy standing at the booking hall and goes to the booking-office window, about twenty feet from where he, White, is standing. The boy moves towards the ticket-collector's barrier and the man calls *"Come you, here."* The man appears to have purchased a ticket as he leaves the office window and rejoins the boy.

White decides to wait a few days before giving information, but meanwhile he forms the impression, from pictures published in the Daily Mirror, that the photographs of the father of the dead boy resemble the man he saw with a boy on the day of the murder. The witness describes certain steps he took to confirm his impression, including a visit he makes to Tottenham Court Road where John sells newspapers to try to identify the man he saw.

In reply to the Jury Foreman, White says that to the best of his belief John was wearing a trilby hat.

"Have you recognised the man you saw?"

"Yes, Sir." White said he recognises him outside Shoreditch Church today.

When asked if he could identify him now by pointing him out in the court, White turns, and points to John.

He says *"That is the gentleman."*

John jumps to his feet and shouts *"It's a lie. It's a damned lie."*

Tilley, who is seated near to John, adds *"So, it is a lie. He was in bed. It must be his double."*

The Jury Foreman asks of White *"Do you recognise his voice?"*

White responds *"Yes; I know the man; I will swear to it."*

"Was the child going willingly with him?"

"Most decidedly. They were most affable together. The man was laughing as they went towards the ticket collector."

"You did not notice whether the child was eating cake?"

"No, I noticed very little of the child."

"You are quite positive of the man?"

"I am."

White is then handed a photograph of Willie and his comment is *"That is the kind of boy I saw Mr Starchfield with."*

White goes on to say that the reason that he did not come forward immediately was because he has endured sleepless nights of worry. After discussing the matter at length with a friend, he feels he must come forward to relieve his mind. It was then that he contacts the Police. White then explains that he met with Chief Inspector Gough at Old Street Police Station. Gough instructs him to follow Detective Inspector Alfred Ball to the vicinity of Shoreditch Coroner's Court where he is informed that he will see several people. If White can identify anyone there, he should communicate this to Ball who always keeps him in view[5].

White relates how he and Ball reach the Court at 1.50pm finding a crowd of approximately 300 people milling around, their numbers increasing as time passes. White walks around within the crowd and, at 2.20pm, walks towards Ball and points out a man unknown to Ball.

He says *"That is the man I saw at Canning Town Station."*

Ball asks him *"Are you sure?"*

White replies *"I am positive, thank God. I am sure I have made no mistake."*

White then describes how he and Ball wait outside the Courthouse, not discussing the case, until 2.45pm whereupon he is taken by Ball to the waiting room of the Courthouse once John is inside. They wait there together until he is called to give evidence just now by the Coroner.

Westcott thanks White for coming forward. He says there seems no reasonable probability of finding more corroborative evidence at present. He observes that unless the Jury makes some suggestion as to the direction in which they should continue researches, that they might conclude the inquiry after hearing evidence from Chief Inspector Gough.

Gough then outlines the investigations which have been made by the Police. He says that the movements of persons upon whom suspicion might have fallen have been exhaustively inquired into. Nevertheless, there is no evidence obtained to connect anyone with the matter up to the present. As far as Gough is concerned there is no evidence which would justify an arrest.

He then relates the history of the Starchfields as a family. Gough details John's army service in the South African War. He explains that John and Agnes marry at St Giles's Registry Office in October 1903. There are three children from the marriage, two of whom die from illness, and Willie. The marriage is not a happy one as they part on many occasions. Six weeks after their marriage, Agnes attends Marlborough Street Police Court to complain about John's treatment of her. As a result of this complaint John is prosecuted, a separation order is granted, and John is ordered to pay her five shillings a week. He persistently fails to comply with this order, which obliges Agnes to earn her living as a Tailoress.

Gough describes further quarrels and separations. He says that after John's involvement in the Titus Tottenham Court Road murder in 1912, Agnes joins him once more. Another separation follows in 1913 and he allows her the £1 a week which he is awarded for six months from the Carnegie Fund. This is reduced to 15 shillings a week, and ends on 1st January this year; he has not since contributed to her maintenance.

Westcott begins his summing up, characterising the suggestion that the crime may have been committed by a friend of Titus in revenge for John's actions in stopping him as *"a very wild notion."* Westcott mentions that the movements of the young male lunatic patient who escaped from Colney Hatch Lunatic Asylum on the 7th January have been traced on his return to the Asylum, and it is quite clear that he has had nothing to do with the boy's murder.

The Police are satisfied about the mother's movements. If John and the people in the lodging-house have sworn falsely, then it is possible that John might have been the man whom Mrs Wood saw in Kentish Town Road, and Mr White saw at Camden Town Station. In short, there is no evidence against anybody unless it was the father. The question for the Jury's consideration to justify them in sending John for trial, is whether there is sufficient evidence. At this point, Westcott clears the court of bystanders apart from the witnesses and the members of the Jury.

The Jury retires for fifty-three minutes. On returning, the Foreman is asked by Westcott if they have come to any decision.

The Foreman replies *"We are unanimous in regarding the evidence of the witnesses called by Mr Starchfield as unreliable, and entirely lacking in corroboration. We are unanimously of the opinion that Starchfield and his principal witness, Tilley, have failed to account satisfactorily for their whereabouts on the afternoon of January 8th 1914. We are unanimous in believing that the man and the child seen by Mrs Wood and Mr White on the afternoon in question were Mr Starchfield and his son, Willie."*

The Jury Foreman pauses before adding*: "It is the wish of the Jury that that should be regarded as a verdict against Starchfield.[6]"*

Westcott asks *"You mean that he should be charged with the wilful murder of his son?"*

The Foreman responds *"That is so."*

Westcott then orders Gough to arrest John for the murder of his son, and he immediately makes out a warrant for John's arrest and detention. At this point, John, who has remained calm during the absence of the Jury making their deliberations, seems dazed by the verdict. Agnes breaks down sobbing.

Gough places his hand on John's shoulder and immediately arrests him for 'Wilful Murder.' When the charge is read over to him John says *"I am innocent of this crime."* He is immediately taken before Mr Biron, the Magistrate, at Old Street Police Court. On hearing the evidence of the charge, Biron remands John into Police custody until 2nd February[7].

CHAPTER FIVE

The Detective

> *"A detective is born, not made, and if a man has not a natural aptitude for unravelling crime, all the rules and regulations for the detection of crime will not make him a detective"* (William Gough, 1936[1]).

Chief Inspector William Gough prefers advancement by merit. Once appointed as a police officer, by 1914 he enjoys a meteoric rise through the ranks in an age when the police force is comprised in the main of working-class men. A strange incident decides Gough's future career. As a boy of fourteen, and the son of a Police Officer at Richmond, he is suddenly sent for by no less a person than Sir William Harcourt, the then Home Secretary. Harcourt lives nearby Gough's family home. Gough nervously presents himself at Harcourt's address and is informed that his name has been given to Sir William as that of a 'reliable boy.' He is to take charge of some books on a journey to London and back. He travels by train and cab to the Home Office, accompanied by the Home Secretary, clasping the books in his arms. On arrival, he is directed to a back room, where he sits all day guarding the precious volumes. He then returns with them to Richmond. The purpose of this assignment remains unclear[2].

During Gough's career, Police recruitment morphs from a 19th century agrarian 'pool' of single men, who tend to leave under a two-year period for better-paid employment, into an early 20th century hard-core of long-serving men. Many of these men are ex-servicemen and there is a steady stream of recruits attracted by regular pay, secure employment, and a pension. By 1907, Peel House in London opens as a training school which elevates the Police as more of a profession. Their pay and conditions may be less than some other professions but their self-perception is that of the skilled workman. Policing is becoming a positive means of employment. It has a hierarchy with rewards for exemplary conduct. Dismissals are low and fall into the categories of drunkenness, insubordination and 'failing to act in the manner befitting a Constable[3].'

Some anti-Police sentiment remains as a hangover from the 19th century handling of public protests, and assaults on Police Officers are not uncommon in a sprawling, urbanised London. Nevertheless, by 1914 there is public support for the Police evidenced by improvements in Policing methods such as fingerprinting. The first British Fingerprint

Bureau is founded at Scotland Yard in 1901 using the Henry Classification System. This was developed in India by Sir Edward Henry, then the Inspector General of Police, in Bengal, India[4].

This is a Great Britain which is mainly mono-cultural but, history records that some black Africans arrive as soldiers in the Roman Army from the 2nd century. From the 1500s onwards, there are some non-white migrants living in the Metropolis[5]. By the 1900s, other minority groups mainly comprised of economic migrants from Europe are vying for employment but are viewed with suspicion in a country poised on the brink of war. There is a view that some of these people are transient migrants using the country to further personal ambitions. Many refugees view returning to their home country as less feasible than remaining *in situ* in a country where they are shunned by the local populace. Domestic politics over-riding foreign policy have passed the Aliens Act in 1905 attempting to end immigrant arrivals[6].

The indigenous, urban, white, working-class poor inhabit and barely exist in this Edwardian world. They scratch a living, whilst the growth of military might is combined with nationalism in Great Britain. The rich own 90% of the nation's wealth. Scientific advances such as photography become more mainstream and photographs of East End inhabitants become common due to prurient interest in the 'slum life' of the working classes. In 1914, little has changed since 1883 when Francis Peek the social commentator writes *"In any dismal alleys and fetid courts of our large towns, the impure and stagnant air depresses and enervates those who return home, already exhausted by work...many families...have only one single room, in which parents and children of all ages and both sexes work, live and sleep.*[7]*"* Radical reform is in the air underpinning the foundations of a fledgling trade union movement brought about by a more politicised working class.

Edward VII is the first monarch to preside over a predominantly urban Britain as a result of the agricultural depression of the 1870s. His 1901 accession ceremony is delayed due to appendicitis, so Buckingham Palace chefs donate the already prepared food to the poor in the East End, a rare concession by the monarchy. Edward's successor in 1910, George V, ushers in a more abstemious and traditionalist age. In a shrewd move in 1917 he will appease British nationalist feelings by renaming the royal house from that of Saxe-Coburg and Gotha to Windsor. Back in 1914 the population of Great Britain, according to the Census, stands at 40,338,867, and Gough and his colleagues police a London that is a 'melting pot' of humanity[8].

Six months prior to Willie's death Gough investigates another death of a child on a railway. The naked body of a two-year-old child is found lying between the rails of the four-foot way on the South-Eastern Railway of England, between Wellington College and Wokingham Stations. The body is first seen by the driver of a goods train at 4.50 am, who alerts authorities at Wokingham Junction. A Platelayer finds the body about an hour later, lying clear of the metals, and places it at the side of the track. It appears that the child has been thrown from a train. The skull, the left arm and leg are fractured and there are severe bruises and abrasions over the right eye and on the left shoulder respectively.

A short distance from the body on the railway line, searchers find a coat of light corded material and a skirt. Three miles nearer Reading is a child's undergarment with the initials "A.F." worked in blue cotton and a cape to match the coat found near the body. Within a mile of Reading station is a child's flannelette petticoat with the letter 'A,' in red cotton, a pair of cloth stays and a woollen vest. All are of poor quality. The supposition is that the child must have been thrown from a 'down' train, owing to the position of the body on the 'up' line.

Information reaches the Police of an attractive-looking woman, aged about twenty years, acting in a suspicious manner in the 7pm train from Charing Cross. The attention of other passengers is attracted to the woman by her conduct near Earley, Reading. It is believed she got out at Reading station. Police enquiries never trace the woman[9]. This case may be a stark reminder to Gough to 'get his man' once he is assigned to the Starchfield Murder Case. In January 1914 the Starchfield Murder Case is highly publicised and the subsequent Inquest and Trial are headline news.

CHAPTER SIX

The Investigation

Following his arrest and charge at the Inquest, thirty-nine-year-old John is remanded in custody on 2nd February 1914. He appears on remand in Court for plea hearings on the 3rd, 4th, and 6th of February, once again appearing before Mr Biron the Magistrate. On each occasion, Mr A. H. Bodkin attends the Court to prosecute on behalf of the Director of Public Prosecutions. Mr Henry Margetts, a Solicitor, is in attendance to conduct John's defence[1].

In outlining the case for the Prosecution, Mr Bodkin places all the current evidence before the Court. His style of delivery is built on a solid appreciation of the facts of the case. He lays out a special stress upon the positive identification of John by Mrs Clara Wood and by Mr White. He details the forensic evidence provided by Dr Spilsbury of the boy's stomach contents, which corroborates Mrs Wood's Inquest evidence. He describes the confirmation by the Booking Clerk at Camden Town Railway Station of the acceptance of Mr White's parcel on 8th January, corroborating Mr White's Inquest evidence that he was there and saw John and his son together[2].

Bodkin concludes by stressing the importance of the evidence from Jackson, the Signalman, who has a clear view from his vantage point in the signal box. Jackson states he sees a man answering to John's description, leaning over the form of either a boy or a girl in the slow-moving Chalk Farm train. Jackson now swears positively that the form over which the man was leaning was that of the deceased boy, whose body he identified at the mortuary as being the same boy on the train[3].

On the 5th February John Moore, a Timber Porter, of 12 Tolmer's Square, Hampstead Road, informs Police that he can give important information relating to John's movements on 8th January. Moore's statement says that he has been acquainted with John for upwards of five years. He asserts that he sees John with a little boy at 1.50pm on the day of the murder outside Camden Town Tube Station in Kentish Town Road. John is going in the direction of Kentish Town, by which way he could go to Camden Town Station (the North London Railway).

The value of this evidence is immediately realised as it is consistent with the evidence of Mrs Wood, Mr White, and Mr Jackson. This evidence effectively tracks the movements of John and his son from

Camden Town Tube Station to the incident on the train as seen by Mr Jackson.

Moore's statement is taken by the Police on the 6th February and he is told to ready himself for an appearance at Old Street Police Court. Mr Bodkin reads through the statement and summons Moore to appear at once at the Courthouse to provide supporting evidence for his statement[4].

Moore appears at the Courthouse as instructed, but due to time constraints John's remand continues. Moore is sent away and is asked to re-appear to give that evidence on the 9th February. At this hearing, he is cross-examined by Margetts at considerable length with a view to prove his evidence is unreliable; having previously made totally different statements to various persons. Moore denies giving other accounts about the matter.

At one point Moore turns to John, who is there in person, and asks *"Don't you know me?"*

John responds *"No, I don't."*

In the witness box Moore comes across as an ignorant and talkative man whose evidence does not assist the case as well as anticipated by the Prosecution team. Nevertheless, Moore is summoned to appear again at the Trial. Meanwhile, John remains remanded in custody with a Trial date set for 31st March 1914. His brother James is his only visitor. This period gives the Police more time to gather further evidence.

CHAPTER SEVEN

The Affidavit

More interest in the Starchfield case is engendered when, between the Inquest and Trial, there are civil proceedings brought before Mr Justice Channell, Mr Justice Scrutton and Mr Justice Bailhache on the 4th March[1]. John's legal team in this matter is led by Mr G.W.H. Jones. These proceedings call upon the Editor of the *Lloyd's Weekly News* to show cause as to why he should not be committed for contempt of the Court for publishing a certain article on 1st March. This article purports to be an Affidavit, signed by Agnes Starchfield, and contains statements prejudicial to John and the upcoming Trial[2]. John's Solicitor moves for a *'rule nisi'* (an order "to show cause" meaning that the ruling is absolute unless the party to whom it applies can show cause why it should not apply).

This Affidavit is headed: *The Murder of Willie Starchfield: His Mother's declaration to Lloyds News.* It begins with a general history of the case, explaining that there can be no objection to this. It then proceeds with Agnes' statement:

"I, Agnes Starchfield, of 191 Hampstead Road, N.W., in the County of London, make oath and say as follows: - There have been so many rumours floating about which have not an atom of foundation, that I want the public to know exactly what took place on the day my little boy was murdered. I want the people to know exactly what I did every minute of the time I was away from home and during the time Willie was lost. The police know all this already, for I made a full statement to them on the very night of the tragedy, but it has not appeared in any newspaper, so I shall let my statement be published in Lloyds Weekly News."

Mr Jones objects to that paragraph. The account of Agnes' movements is of great importance to his client, he declares. He does not read it out but raises an objection to a following paragraph within the statement: *"She replied to my remark: 'Oh, no; he's been gone since a quarter to one' and with that she burst out crying. Then I realised that he was really lost."*

Another paragraph is objected to:

"I knew that that was only a faint chance, because Willie wouldn't speak to a stranger, and wouldn't go with anybody. He didn't know any children about here, because he was never allowed in the street unless there was someone grown up with him."

This is very prejudicial to John because it is calculated to limit the area of suspicion by pointing to someone well acquainted with Willie, such as his father. The statement also says that Willie would not speak to a stranger.

The pre-Trial defence that had been opened on John's behalf is that, according to witnesses, the child was last seen with a woman. They were going in the direction of Camden Road, and then went by an omnibus to a place near Chalk Farm Station.

The last paragraph of the statement is:

"We went to Old Street, where Chief Inspector Gough asked me to describe all my movements during the day. These I told him, as I have recounted them to you today. Then we went to the mortuary, where my landlady identified the body, and the detective afterwards took us home. When we were living in Chitty Street, Willie once went with another boy to see the pictures. Another time I found him in a cinema and brought him out, telling him: 'You naughty boy. What have you come here for?'

With regard to the proceedings in court I cannot say anything until the case is over and then I can absolutely justify my position and everything I have said. I can say that there has never been a better mother on this earth, not only to my child Willie, but to the two others."

The statement is signed by Agnes and purports to have been sworn by a Commissioner for Oaths.

At the Inquest it is evidenced that John is in his bed at his lodgings until the afternoon on the day of the murder. This is confirmed in evidence by a person named Tilley, a fellow lodger. This evidence is rebutted by Agnes when recalled to give evidence by the Coroner. She says that she saw Tilley in the street on that day.

Mr Justice Channell remarks *"You ought to prosecute the Commissioner who purported to take the oath. There is nothing in the statement except what has been said over and over. You cannot stop publicity."*

In response, Mr Jones says that he is not trying to stop publicity, but he is trying to stop trial by newspapers. Agnes has given a complete history of her movements on this day, and this ought not to have been published in a newspaper. The statement has been very widely circulated while the Inquest was proceeding. It is a statement by a woman who could not be called to give evidence and could not be cross-examined.

Mr Justice Channell says that a rule will be granted. He wishes to say that he has a strong feeling that applications to commit for contempt of the Court ought to be discouraged. The present case, however, is a comment on a serious criminal case, and that makes a considerable difference. The statement purports to be an Affidavit. He believes that it is quite wrong for a Commissioner to take an oath of that kind.

In addition, it purports to be a statement on oath by a person who could not give evidence on oath before a Jury. Therefore, it seems to him to be a publication by a newspaper of a statement which may be prejudicial to the prisoner. This statement has been made by a person who is not admissible as a witness. On those grounds he believes that the rule should be granted.

Mr Jones afterwards applies to have the hearing of the rule expedited.

Mr Justice Channel says that the fact that the rule has been granted will protect the applicant from any further comments. If it were necessary for John's protection the Court would expedite the Trial hearing, but as it was, he thinks that it may come on in the ordinary course.

Mr Justice Scrutton says that this newspaper, as well as other newspapers, will take note of the fact that the rule had been granted. The court therefore refuses to expedite the Trial hearing which remains scheduled to commence on the 31st March at the Old Bailey.

CHAPTER EIGHT

The Father: 8th January 1914

In the early morning of the 8th January 1914, John Starchfield is asleep in his cot in a miserable, multi-occupancy dwelling house at 12 Hanover Court in Longacre. It is a half hour walk from St Pancras South, which was once dubbed 'the foulest parish in all London.' The area remains grim, attracting the philanthropic attention of social reporters following in the footsteps of Charles Booth[1]. Foggy London attracts immigrants who take up residence within its alleyways and narrow streets. Attempting to earn a living, they rub shoulders with the 'born Cockneys,' but are never quite accepted.

In the 19th century nations fiercely guard their borders. Great Britain remains a mighty island sovereign state, its tentacles stretching worldwide, and determined to keep its status as a world power. Many Russian Jewish immigrants find themselves subject to pogroms in their homeland following the assassination of Tsar Alexander II in 1881 and seek sanctuary elsewhere. Jewish people migrating from East to West for a new life are generally viewed with suspicion. In January 1905 an Aliens Act is passed to restrict immigration with a remit to target 'undesirables.[2]'

From his early years in a working-class family, John has led a peripatetic existence, fending for himself and his brother James, who works on the railway. In 1897 he describes himself as a Newsvendor on his voluntary Militia Infantry Attestation form[3]. He is glad to sign up for the meagre pay that supplements his wages. On the 8th August 1899, on his Army Short Service form[4], John is a twenty-year-old man who describes his occupation as a 'labourer'. The form describes him as 5' 5" in height, weighing 121 lbs, with a 32-and-a-half-inch chest, with hazel eyes, and brown hair. He is a single man who has never been apprenticed. John signs his name in the presence of Mr H. M. Rowland, a Magistrate, to confirm he agrees to Her Majesty's conditions of service.

In 1901 he signs up again to serve in the Second Boer War. This dispute centres upon the Afrikaner farmers, or Boers, who are intent on rural independence in the wake of British settlers and miners who arrive following the discovery of gold on the Rand. For John, Army service, even in the Orange Free State of an unknown South Africa, provides him with a more stable existence of regular food and accommodation.

As a British Infantryman sweating under the South African sun, John is dressed in his lighter weight khaki drill uniform of the 4th Battalion Kings' Royal Rifles. His Lee-Enfield rifle is primed ready for action, John bites off the top of the cartridge, fills it with gunpowder and drops in the bullet. A bayonet spike or 'pig sticker' is attached to the muzzle. His date clasps are attached to his cap but he will go bare-headed in the bright sunshine. His cap insignia makes him an easy target for any Boer marksman. The Boers regularly outmanoeuvre the British soldiers with their effective marksmanship and extensive knowledge of the terrain in the gold-rich territories of South Africa. They are bent on revenge since the British burned down Boer farms making their occupants homeless[5].

The British have rounded up 160,000 Boer women and children, corralling them into outdoor prisons known as concentration camps. The Boers are commandos: guerrilla fighters with an arsenal of German weaponry who have spent their lives farming and hunting. They have the psychological advantage of ambush against the military-trained British and regularly blow-up British supply lines in retaliation. The Treaty of Vereeniging that marks the end to the Second Boer War is signed on 31st May 1902 before King Edward VII is crowned in August 1902. The change of Sovereign ushers in a supposed more enlightened age and John and his comrades are discharged back to England[6].

John has gone from hero to zero since being discharged from active service in May 1902, although he remains on the reserve list. He marries Agnes Lineham in 1903 on return from the war, having met her five years previously. Their marriage is dysfunctional and they separate and reunite several times due to John's alcohol dependence and related violence towards Agnes. His Army service record shows that he is sentenced by the Civil Police to three months hard labour as a Reserve Volunteer runaway; having left his wife and child in 1909[7].

In 1910, John is sentenced again to three months hard labour. His service record shows that he was convicted by the Police for deserting his wife and child; leaving Agnes and baby Willie 'being chargeable to the parish[8]'. John is finally discharged from Army service in 1911. To make ends meet he becomes a Newsvendor, one of the publications he sells is *John Bull,* a platform for the populist views of Horatio Bottomley, Member of Parliament.

Nonetheless, John becomes a hero again at 11am on Friday 27th September 1912[9]. He is on his way to a public house, the 'Horseshoe Hotel' in Great Russell Street. John views a man standing unsteadily on the doorstep with the sun glinting on the revolver in his hand. There is screaming coming from inside the public house. Unknown to John inside the bar all is carnage. The occupants are dead, dying or wounded.

Out on the street, the man fires a random shot. Ignoring his own safety, John runs at him in a selfless act to knock the revolver from the stranger's hand; he is pre-programmed to protect others due to his military training. The gunman takes aim at John but the gun misfires. John stands his ground. Again, the gunman shoots at John before John can attempt to disarm him. The bullet enters John's abdomen and he collapses on the ground, losing consciousness. The gunman is later identified as an Armenian, Stephen Titus.

Titus is disarmed by George Alfred Holding, a Furniture Porter and Edward Charles Bedding, a Chemist's Assistant, both having been caught in the cross-fire of shots from Titus who deliberately fires his revolver at them. They hold on to Titus to assist Police Constable Abbs until Police Constable Saunders arrives. Saunders then walks Titus to Tottenham Court Road Police Station. Titus' response on being charged is *"I don't remember."* He is remanded in custody.

On 5th November 1912 at the Old Bailey, Titus, a Tailor by trade, is indicted and charged on Coroner's inquisition with the wilful murder of Esther May

Towers and Thomas Morris Johns. He is indicted for feloniously wounding Grace Rachael Ray, Charles Hook, and John, in each case with intent to murder. Titus, when called upon to plead, remains mute. A Jury is sworn to try whether the prisoner stands mute of malice.

Sidney Reginald Dyer, the Principal Medical Officer at Brixton Prison, testifies that Titus understands English and has no problems with his hearing. Dyer says that *"Now and again he has been in a morose condition. I saw him before he came to the court this morning and he was in that condition then. He is in the same condition now, but he quite understands, and I think he is fit to plead and follow the course of the trial and give the necessary instructions for his defence."* The Jury finds that the prisoner stands mute of malice. Mr Justice Phillimore directs a plea of Not Guilty to be entered on each indictment, and requests that Mr Waldo Briggs, Solicitor, represent Titus.

On Monday 11th November the witnesses for the Trial prosecution are sworn in. Their testimonies are sobering and distressing. Police Constable George Henry Towers relates *"I saw the body of my sister, Esther May Towers, at St Giles' mortuary. She was employed at the 'Horseshoe Hotel' as assistant manageress."*

Grace Rachel Ray, a Barmaid at the 'Horseshoe Hotel', depicts the scene when Miss Towers was shot. She says *"I knew the prisoner by sight. He used to come into the bar at 11 o'clock in the morning and have some refreshment; he was very silent... Miss Towers attended to him... My attention was not on the prisoner. I next heard a report, and I thought it was outside; it sounded like a tyre bursting. I then heard two more sharp reports. When I heard the last report, I was looking at Miss Towers...I only heard three reports. I saw Miss Towers kneeling down. I went to assist her and she fell down, and I fell down too. I found afterwards that I had been shot in the shoulder; I fainted."*

John Charles Picking, a Manufacturers Agent recounts *"I was in the coffee-bar at the 'Horseshoe Hotel' with Mr Johns...I saw the prisoner there...Mr Johns and I were sitting at a table at the end of the bar. While sitting there I heard the report of a pistol; I heard five or six in quick succession; they came from the direction in which the prisoner was standing. I saw blood on Mr John's face. I ducked down by the side of the table. Prisoner ran out of the bar. Mr Johns was taken to hospital, and has since died."*

William Henry Mick, a Waiter at the 'Horseshoe Hotel' corroborates the previous statements thus *"On this morning I was in the bar; I saw the prisoner standing in the bar and Miss Towers and Miss Wray* serving. I heard a report, which sounded to me as if an electric globe had fallen down. I was standing at the entrance to the bar. I turned round and saw the prisoner fire at Miss Wray; he then turned round and fired at Mr Pickering and Mr Johns. He fired once towards where I was standing and ran up to the bar; I ran out of the bar. I heard some more firing in the street."

Police Constable Bertie Abbs states "A little after 11 o'clock on the morning of September 27th I heard pistol shots coming from the direction of Great Russell Street. I went to Great Russell Street and saw prisoner standing on the footway shooting at random with a revolver in his right hand. I saw Starchfield approach prisoner and attempt to knock the revolver out of his hand; prisoner chased Starchfield and fired at him. I heard the revolver click; it had missed fire; Starchfield still went for prisoner; prisoner took aim and shot Starchfield in the abdomen; I saw him fall on the pavement. I saw Holding make a rush at prisoner from the front and tried to arrest him; I closed with him from behind. I seized his wrist and took the revolver from him. There were no cartridges in it then."

Cross-examination of all the witnesses by Mr Briggs for the defence is concise and is aimed at eliciting whether the prisoner was provoked by the witnesses. Sidney Reginald Dyer, the Principal

Medical Officer at Brixton Prison is recalled to the stand to give his opinion on Titus' mental state.

He opines *"I have had several prolonged interviews with him. He was rather incoherent, but he gave me a fairly lucid account of himself and his life. He told me he was born in Turkey and that at the age of 17 he went to America to join his family, who had preceded him; that for the last four years he had been bothered by everyone, first his parents and then by others; that this persecution gradually became more extended to people he did not know and which he vaguely referred to as 'they'; he said they tried to poison him; he had moved from place to place, seeking solitude and to escape his tormentors; that they still pursued him; he intended to return to his native country via London and Paris; he tried to get a ticket to Turkey from Cook's; they could not book him through on account of the railway strike; he got the delusion into his head that Cook's people had also joined the conspiracy against him, so he returned to London and stayed at the 'Horseshoe Hotel'. He said that they all tormented him, even the barmaids, by poisoning the food, cigars, etc., to make his brain give way. He said he had nothing to do with anyone.*

When I saw him on his arrival at Brixton, he was very violent and made rambling statements about being followed about. The next day, after a prolonged sleep, he quieted down and has since behaved well. He is entirely indifferent to his surroundings, speaks to no one, and has no signs of remorse. He has no recollection whatever of the events happening at the time of the crime. These symptoms are typical of delusional insanity. I think when he shot the barmaid, he might have known he was shooting, but I do not think he was capable of forming any sound judgement; he certainly did not know the quality of his act. He probably thought it was right."

Under further cross-examination, Dyer continues *"His condition has altered whilst he has been in prison; he has been much quieter; the last few days he has been very sullen and morose and has refused to answer questions at all. In my opinion he was insane at the time of committing the act. I do not think he was shamming."*

The verdict is Guilty, but insane at the time of the commission of the offence. Titus is ordered to be detained at His Majesty's pleasure[10].

At the conclusion of the Trial, John is awarded £50 by the Judge and, in 1913, John is recognised by the Carnegie Hero Fund for his bravery. The Fund has been established in 1908 to recognise civilian heroism and provide financial assistance to injured heroes and their dependants. Andrew Carnegie, the founder of the fund, states *"The false heroes of barbarous man are those who can only boast of the destruction of their fellows. The true heroes of civilisation are those alone who save or greatly save them."*

John is awarded an honorary certificate and an allowance of £1 a week for six months. At the end of this period, he is awarded a further allowance of 15s a week for six months, but the award finishes in January 1914[11]. Having enjoyed the monetary benefits of the award, he once more faces an uncertain future of irregular earnings and ill-health.

The money is a constant source of contention between John and Agnes, because it is expected by her that he should provide a portion of it for her and Willie. The fact that this award money has ended the week prior to Willie's death, arouses Gough's suspicions about John's alibi and is heavily scrutinised by him.

CHAPTER NINE

Day One of the Trial: 31st March 1914,
The Old Bailey Court, London

The newspapers' headlines have dubbed the case as 'The North London Railway Murder,' 'The Train Murder,' or the 'Starchfield Case.' Press interest is high for any murder Trial because conviction carries the death sentence, so the Trial will be intensively reported for the delectation of its readers. Horatio Bottomley, who is the newspaper proprietor of the *John Bull* publication, is paying for John's legal defence team. Bottomley's stirring defence of John as one of his Newsvendors within his editorial concentrates upon John's war record and subsequent heroism in the Titus affair. Bottomley's proud boast is that *John Bull's* motto is – politics without party – criticism without cant – and without fear or favour, rancour, or rant.

On 21st February 1914, *John Bull* runs an article with the heading 'Who is Starchfield?[1]' It answers its own question by briefly describing John as a *'British subject and by trade a street newspaper seller.'* It underpins human interest in the case by representing John as belonging to *'that class of rough, honest fellows upon whom our sales considerably depend.'* Bottomley prides himself on being a defender of the working man's right to be informed of up-to-the-minute news. He garners a significant readership by using a magazine-type format using a mixture of advertisements, readers' letters, campaigns, and editorial pieces. This type of newspaper coverage produces a groundswell of interest in the murder and thus a substantial public attendance at the trial.

Early in the morning of 31st March a queue forms in Newgate Street outside the Old Bailey in London. Members of the public wait for the 9.00am opening of the side door to the public gallery of Court Number One, the principal English Criminal Court, to view this noteworthy Trial. Some late arrivals are members of the press corps who have paid individuals to take their places in the queue. On admittance to the public gallery, observers sit under arches supporting a circular skylight of plain glass. Two rows of seats behind Counsel are occupied by fashionable ladies, eager for diversion in their lives[2].

The 'new' Old Bailey has been open since 1907[3]. This Central Criminal Court building is built upon the site of the old Newgate Prison and the former Old Bailey building. Within its walls in 1910 Hawley Harvey Crippen and, in 1912, Frederick Seddon are both tried in Court Number One, and subsequently hanged. As a matter of routine, Bernard Spilsbury is called as a pathologist to give evidence in both cases. Today, Spilsbury attends John's Trial as an expert witness, as does Dr Garrett the Police Surgeon who originally examined Willie's body.

John is brought up into the dock via well-worn steps from the plethora of cells beneath containing other defendants awaiting trial. He stands as straight as his previous military training allows during proceedings, even though his wound from the Titus incident continues to pain him. The dock dominates the courtroom, which is uncommonly small. John, not the tallest of men, is dwarfed by the dock's structure; but he finds himself at eye-level with the rostered Judge, Mr Justice Atkin, who sits off-centre. The seating is a peculiarity of this courtroom: this is due to the centre seat being the ancient prerogative of the Lord Mayor of London, who only attends the court for ceremonial purposes. The witnesses, when called, will face Counsel, and will be heard clearly by the Judge.

A few weeks previously, Justice Atkin is the Trial Judge in the February 1914 Liverpool case of Ball and Eltoft (the 'sack' murder)[4]. Ball is hanged for murder and Eltoft receives a four-year sentence for disposing of a body. It is reported that "Atkin *saw issues in terms of clear and definite dividing lines. He exemplified this by his strong belief in the separation of powers between executive, legislature, and judiciary."* Atkin's closing remarks at the end of John's Trial underline his stance on judicial processes.

The raised Jury bench, containing the twelve men who are already sworn in, runs the full width of the Courtroom. They are drawn from a 'respectable' lower middle class who are expected to decide the case fairly and without bias. John's military background and heroism will be in his favour in the all-male Jury room. John is sworn in, but there is a pause in proceedings. A Juryman now raises his hand and tells the Judge that he is strongly opposed to capital punishment. He requests that he be allowed to leave the service on the Jury[5].

Judge Atkin asks *"Have you had those views for some time?"*

The man replies *"Yes, for many years."*

Atkin responds *"I do not think you are a desirable juryman to have on a capital charge.*

You had better go."

The man leaves the Jury bench and is immediately replaced by another man. Mr Bodkin then proceeds to open the case for the Prosecution.

When asked to plead John says *"not guilty"* in a loud voice. He is seated between two warders and listens attentively to the case against him, his black hair is now tinged with grey. Bodkin reminds the Jurors that they must cast from their minds anything that they have heard or read about the case. They must only decide upon the facts as presented in this Courtroom.

Bodkin outlines the case for the Prosecution, describing Willie's movements on the day of the murder: the resultant search by his mother and her landlady, and the discovery of the boy's body on the train and the marks on his neck. He describes the deceased child as attractive with long, curly brown hair and the only surviving child of John and Agnes Starchfield. Bodkin then relates John's association with the Titus case and his bravery award, detailing the amount of money that John was awarded by the Carnegie Fund: initially £1 a week which is then reduced to 15 shillings a week after six months. This award money ceases in January 1914 as the award was for one year only.

Bodkin continues with a description of the North London Railway train service that day, suggesting that the body laid undiscovered from approximately 1.30pm until its discovery by George Tillman who had climbed into that particular carriage. He informs the court that Mr White, a commercial traveller, will state that at about 2pm he sees the prisoner with a boy in the booking hall at Camden Town Station. The man buys a ticket for the North London Railway which is 400 yards from the tube station.

Bodkin reads from a statement by a Signalman called Jackson. He was looking out from his signal box for a shunting operation which took place at eight minutes past 2pm. This was the very time that the 1.59pm train from Chalk Farm passed. In the carriage at the back of the train where the body was found he saw the head and shoulders of a man and the head of a curly headed person moving to and fro. He initially cannot say whether it was a boy or a girl, but he has seen the body of the strangled boy. He identifies the head on the boy's body as that of Willie Starchfield. He is unable to identify the man.

> Looking at the Jury, Bodkin continues, *"The opinion of the skilled mind is that when the cord had been tightened round his neck the boy would probably have died within a minute. The medical evidence is that the boy died between two and three o' clock that afternoon of strangulation."*

Allowing the Jury to process this information, Bodkin reminds the Court of the events at the Coroner's Court. He regurgitates John's outburst of denial when witnesses assert that they saw him with his son. He recounts how Mrs Clara Wood comments on the murdered boy enjoying a cake in the street near Anglers Lane. She identifies the man accompanying the boy as John. A shop nearby is known to sell similar cakes containing coconut. This tallies with the post mortem report of a half-digested cake in the boy's stomach.

Bodkin explains how this shop is approximately 2,150 yards from the boy's home at 191 Hampstead Road. In corroboration of this statement, he produces a Police report dated the 19th March, authorised by Chief Inspector Gough. This early spatial report of intelligence gathering, has its roots in Charles Booths' contemporary neighbourhood classifications of the London poverty maps.

In this report PC Attersoll provides the following statement[6]:

> "As directed, I have walked the distance between No 12 Hanover Court, Long Acre, W.C., and the various places named herein with regard to which I give the times and distances: -

> From 12 Hanover Court to 191 Hampstead Road, N.W. The distance is 2,480 yards and time taken to walk same at slightly under 3 miles per hour was 30 minutes.

> From 191 Hampstead Road to Anglers Lane, N.W., the distance is 2,150 yards and the time taken to

walk same at slightly under 3 miles per hour was 24 minutes.

From Anglers Lane, N.W., To Camden Town Underground Station at junction of Camden Road and Kentish Town Road is 943 yards and the time taken to walk at rate as above was 12 minutes.

From Camden Town Underground Station to North London Railway Station at junction of Great College Street and Camden Road is 400 yards and time taken at above rate 5 minutes.

The total distance covered is 3 miles 693 yards and the total time taken to walk same was 1 hour 11 minutes.

I commenced to walk the route at 12.45pm on 17th March 1914 starting from 12 Hanover Court and arrived at 191 Hampstead Road at 1.15pm, thence to Anglers Lane arriving at 1.39pm thence to Camden Town Underground Station arriving at 1.51pm then to North London Railway Station, Camden Town, arriving there at 1.57pm. I have worked out the rate of walking which averages slightly under 3 miles per hour, viz: 5973 yards divided by 62.12 yards per minute or 2 miles, 1400 yards per hour."

Returning to Mrs Wood's eyewitness identification, Bodkin surmises that John appears to have retraced his steps. At this point John is identified by a man named Moore, a Porter, who knew him some years previously. Moore's evidence states that he sees John with a boy at 1.45pm close to the Camden Town tube station, 960 yards from Anglers Lane. John is wearing a dark cap and Moore recounts that he acknowledged John, who tugs his cap over his eyes in response. Bodkin turns towards John in the dock and points at him dramatically. Bodkin suggests that the crime was committed on the train itself. His theory is that the perpetrator could have taken a tube at Broad Street station and have been in the West End by 3pm[7].

Emily Longstaff, the landlady, is then called to give evidence and explains that she sent Willie out on an errand. She was in 'loco parentis' of Willie. Mr Hemmerde comments *"old enough to be sent out on an errand, but not old enough to be left alone in the house?"* In answer to the Judge, the witness says that she has had charge of the boy before.

The next witness, Clara Wood, relates her original evidence at the Inquest. She states that she saw the child, Willie, eating a currant cake in Kentish Town Road. *"He took a bite; his little nose went into it, and he looked up into the man's face and laughed."*

Mr Bodkin: *"Did the man smile at all?"*

"No, he took no notice of the child."

Mrs Wood repeated that she had identified John at the Inquest.

Counsel asked *"Are you absolutely certain that was the man?"*

"Yes, Sir."

"Can you see him here now?"

"Yes, Sir," *looking across at the accused.*

Counsel*: "Is that the man you saw with the boy?"*

"I honestly believe it is." Mrs Wood describes the clothes both were wearing, but she cannot remember whether the man was wearing a soft felt hat.

Bodkin, picking up on this point, observes that different witnesses possess different capacities in remembering details, pointing out that witness statements are recollections, but this does not make them any less true. He makes the point that Mrs Wood says that the prisoner was wearing a soft, felt hat. Moore says it was a cap, White, a dark trilby; and Jackson is convinced the man he saw was wearing a dark bowler hat.

Bodkin now asks Mrs Wood when she first realised the significance of this sighting. She replies *"January 13th."* She adds that she eventually contacts the Police on January 16th and that she did not see any photographs in the newspapers prior to that date.

After she had been to the Police, she sees a photograph of the prisoner and is struck by his likeness with that of the man she had seen leading a little boy by the hand. She admits that she fails to identify the child when initially shown photographs by the Police. Her reason is that she wants to be sure of her identification. She denies having seen more than one photograph of the prisoner before January 22nd. She is then asked if she is short-sighted and says no. She did not notice that the man with the child was lame[8].

Mr Hemmerde, cross-examining, asks *"Before you had heard some other person say it was a cap, you said you thought it was a soft felt hat?"*

"Yes."

Mrs Wood is asked if she had heard that there was a £500 reward for information.

She responds, *"Not before the reporter called on me and I said not for £10,500 would I tell anybody."*

Mrs Wood continues: *"I thought I was giving evidence to catch a lunatic. There was a lunatic at large. The man looked pale like a lunatic. I think he was a lunatic, as he was pale-skinned."*

"Did you think that the man you saw with a boy on the 8th had mad eyes?"

"I don't know."

"Was that what made you think he was a lunatic?"

"I concluded it to myself, and wondered if it was the lunatic."

"Did you think the man you had seen looked like a lunatic?"

"He did not look pleasant-looking. He was frowning and pale. His eyes looked fixed."

She states that he looked Italian-looking.

Mr Bodkin says that in the paper which the Police show to the witness, the portrait of the prisoner appears between two photographs of the boy. The photograph of the prisoner stands out prominently.

"I solemnly swear that I did not look at the portrait of that man. I was so interested in the child."

"What is there about the prisoner that makes you feel so certain?"

She replies, *"His moustache and the expression on his face."*

Further questioning elicits from Mrs Wood that at the Inquest her evidence is read over to her, but she does not sign her statement until the following day. Next day a typewritten copy is given to her in which she makes a correction before signing it.

Mr Bodkin asks if this had been brought to the attention of the Jury. Mrs Wood responds that she does not know.

The Judge observes that this procedure at the Inquest is most irregular and the sooner it is discontinued the better. The dispositions should be signed before the Coroner, who is responsible for their authenticity.

Mr Bodkin states that the Coroner did not take depositions but simply read the statements made to Police Officers by the witnesses.

The Judge comments that all this was extremely unsatisfactory.

Mr Hemmerde makes the point that not only had the Coroner read out the statements made by the Police Officers, but that they had been produced without any cross-examination. The Inquest Jury had then made a verdict against his client.

John Moore takes the stand and reiterates his sighting of John on the day of the murder. Hemmerde, for the defence, informs the Jury that Moore did not report this sighting to the Police until 4th February. He moves to show that there had been some events that would shed light on the reasons for Moore coming forward. Moore has approached a journalist at the offices of the *John Bull* newspaper.

This is with a view to obtaining a pecuniary advantage in exchange for relating his alleged sighting of John with his son on the day of the murder. In corroboration, a spokesman for *John Bull* has given a full statement of the facts to the Police. He relates how Moore was turned away drunk from their offices without a penny being handed over to him.

Hemmerde accuses Moore of not knowing John, and that his story is an invention to gain a pecuniary advantage from the offered reward. Moore denies this and says he was at first frightened to come forward as he was in fear of his life. Hemmerde continues that on March 9th, Moore is found insensible on his bed with a tube in his mouth which is connected to the gas tap. Consequently, on March 26th, a Magistrate bound over Moore in the sum of £5 for attempting to commit suicide. On the witness stand, Moore's reason for this act is that he has been hounded by persons unknown because he had been called to give evidence in the case.

Moore is stood down as it is now 5pm and the Court rises until tomorrow.

CHAPTER TEN

Interest in the Trial remains unabated, and the public gallery is once again full of spectators. The first witness, Dr Garrett, who carried out the initial post mortem examination, explains his findings to the Court[1]. In cross-examination by Mr Margetts, John's Solicitor, Garret relates that he examined the boy's body at 4.40pm on the 8th January. He fixes the probable time of death at two to three hours earlier. It might possibly have occurred between 3.15pm and 3.30pm. He does not apply a thermometer.

> Margetts posits to Garrett *"the murder could have been committed by a woman as easily as a man?"*
>
> Garrett causes a stir in the packed Courtroom by replying *"I see no reason why not."*

Re-examined by Bodkin for the Prosecution, Garrett elaborates upon his previous evidence, but says that it would have been difficult for a woman wearing a tight skirt to have produced certain bruises on the boy's body.

Margetts elicits from Chief Inspector Gough, who is called as the final witness, that several people had viewed the boy's body in the mortuary. Margetts poses the question to Gough that some of these people have given evidence to the effect that they had seen the boy with a woman on the day of his death.

Gough responds *"They said so."*

Margetts pounces upon this asking *"They said so positively? If you allege that it was a man, I am going to show, I hope, that it was a woman."*

Margetts continues *"Was Starchfield most ready and anxious to give you every information that he possibly could?"*

Gough replies *"I should not like to answer that question."*

Re-examined by Bodkin, Gough recalls how he asked John if he would accompany him to Bow Street Police Station on the morning following the murder.

Bodkin inquires *"Did he ask you any questions as to why you were making the inquiries?"*

"No, Sir. I asked him whether he knew the object of the question and he replied in the negative. I then said your son Willie is dead. Starchfield did not say much apart from 'Oh.' He did not seem much moved."

Margetts asks *"At all?"*

Gough replies *"After I had told him that his son had been murdered in a railway carriage on the North London railway, Starchfield showed some slight emotion saying "Has he?" "*

Gough amplifies this by saying that he does not believe that John had been drinking prior to this encounter.

Mr Justice Atkin now addresses Mr Bodkin. He asks him whether he thinks there is a case for the Jury, as he cannot rule that there is no evidence but the case rests entirely upon doubtful identification by three persons. Two of whom state that they have never seen the prisoner before January 8th and one of whom said that she had only seen the prisoner for a moment in passing on that day. Moreover, the evidence of these witnesses differs in their accounts of the clothing that John is alleged to be wearing when they see him. His Honour states that the Jury will need firm evidence upon which to come to a verdict.

Bodkin responds that it is impossible for Counsel not to form views as to the reliability, as distinguished from the honesty, of the witnesses they called. He, himself, is concerned that the case cannot be proven beyond reasonable doubt. Having heard his Lordship's expression of opinion, he states that the Prosecution will withdraw from the case. There are gasps from the Public Gallery, whether disbelief or relief, is unknown. Individuals in the Public Gallery stand up to hear His Honour's closing remarks and dismissal of the case. John leans forward eager to hear every word. Mr Justice Atkin addresses the Jury upon the matter of beyond reasonable doubt. The Jury, after a hurried consultation between them, return a verdict of not guilty[2]. Atkin turns to John and says *"You are free to go."* John remains in the dock to listen to Atkin's further comments as His Honour is not finished.

Atkin is fulsome in his condemnation of both the Police action and the action of the Coroner's Court, which has led to the breakdown of the case for the Crown. He states that the procedure at the Inquest on the dead boy has violated all the principles upon which such an enquiry should be conducted: an enquiry involving the arraignment of a man on a capital charge. Statements of the witnesses that had been taken by Police Officers were read out to them instead of them being asked questions. Furthermore, the witnesses did not sign their depositions at that time, but typewritten copies were sent out to them all over London for their signatures. In some cases, these depositions were then altered by the witnesses in their own homes[3].

Atkin says that such procedures seem to him to be a mockery of due process. He says that the way that the case was conducted in the Coroner's Court made a mockery of justice. Furthermore, the way in which the case has collapsed has dealt a bitter blow to Willie's mother. It has left hanging in the air the unspoken question of who did murder the unfortunate boy, if it was not his father.

Once outside the court, John, leaning heavily on his stick with the support of a friend exits the Court via the Newgate Street door. A crowd of several hundred people gather on hearing the news of the case dismissal. John is chased down the street, and shelters in a doorway. The Police arrive to control the mob of people who wish to congratulate John, and pat him on the back. A taxi is hailed, and he drives off to cries of *"Good old Jack.*[4]*"*

CHAPTER ELEVEN

The Revolutionist

Chief Inspector William Gough is a contemporary of Inspector John Syme. Syme is a 'Policeman's Policeman,' having risen through the ranks to the post of Inspector in the Metropolitan Police. Four years earlier, Syme is dismissed from the Metropolitan Police for alleged insubordination following his support for two of his Officers by speaking up in their defence following a mistaken arrest. He alleges that his colleagues were dealt with too harshly. In the aftermath, Syme is accused of being too familiar with his men and is transferred to a station fourteen miles from his home. He protests this decision and refuses to transfer, at which point he is demoted to the rank of Station Sergeant. He appeals against his sanction to the Commissioner of the Metropolitan Police, Sir Edward Henry, but it is rejected[1].

Syme now begins a lengthy public campaign protesting about his victimisation; he alleges that there is widespread corruption and tyranny within the Metropolitan Police Force. In one instance, he alleges that some Police Officers in 'B' division who were witnesses on his behalf in the complaint against him have been punished and transferred for supporting him. Syme continues to argue his case and becomes a dissident figure who clandestinely founds the National Union of Police and Prison Officers in 1913[2]. He becomes infamous in radical circles, continually waging a campaign for his re-instatement as a Police Officer. He publishes a pamphlet entitled *'Fighting Officialdom, Metropolitan Police Discipline, Has an injustice been done[3]?'* The Union's focus is not on pay and conditions; it concentrates upon exposing the mistreatment of officers and is banned by the Commissioner.

Not content with waging war against the Police, Syme makes allegations against public figures. He posts a notice in the *Daily Herald* urging members of the public to come to Trafalgar Square on Sunday July 20th 1913 to hear speakers debate *'the martyrdom of Lloyd George,'* whom Syme claims is falsely representing himself as a martyr while supporting persecution.

Syme's actions result in a 'revolving door' of prison, hunger strikes, release and then re-arrest and return to prison. In 1913 the Prisoners Temporary Discharge for Ill-Health Act is passed in Parliament, and is often referred to as the 'Cat and Mouse Act.[4]'

This Act allows for the early release of prisoners who are so weakened by hunger striking that they are at risk of death. They are recalled to prison once their health recovers, where the process begins again.

Eventually, Syme loses support from his contemporaries, who oust him from his post as Union secretary due to his notoriety. The Union continues to meet covertly during World War One, but their meetings are monitored by Special Branch. This section of the Metropolitan Police is originally formed in response to an escalating terror campaign in Britain carried out by the militant Irish Fenians in the 1880s. Its objective is counter-terrorism, and is established by the Home Secretary, Sir William Harcourt. He envisions a permanent unit dedicated to the prevention of politically motivated violence, using modern techniques such as undercover infiltration[5].

The Starchfield case attracts Syme's attention, and becomes grist to his radical narrative. By coincidence, on the day of Willie's death, Superintendent Kitch, in a formal statement of rebuttal, states that *"...no officer of any rank has been punished and transferred in consequence of having given evidence on Syme's behalf or for being on his list of witnesses."* Kitch submits to Syme a list of officers who were allegedly punished by transfer with an explanation of the valid reasons for their transfer. This does not sit well with Syme[6].

In a public speech in Hyde Park on 7th May 1914, in the aftermath of the collapse of John's Trial, and his subsequent discharge, Syme makes allegations against Sir Edward Henry. Syme alleges that Henry has supported Chief Inspector Gough in the suppression of evidence of John's innocence during the Trial proceedings. Syme's public allegations against Gough in the days following the conclusion of the Starchfield Trial call into question Gough's professional conduct. This results in an enquiry by his superiors.

On 26th June 1914, Superintendent McCarthy is assigned the duty of producing a report for Henry which details the facts of what Henry terms is an 'unfounded allegation.' McCarthy turns over the request to Gough who produces a three-page typewritten report defending his actions during his investigation into the Starchfield case. McCarthy's handwritten addendum to Gough's report states *"Submitted. There was no suppression of evidence, every little [sic] of information we possessed was passed on to the proper authority, and Starchfield was dealt with most fairly, as was admitted by his solicitor. Mr Syme appears to have jumped at a hasty conclusion without any knowledge of the facts, and has not since had the moral courage to withdraw what he must now know to be an unfounded charge.[7] "*

In July 1914, Syme is in court for the printing and publishing of documents alleging criminal libel against Henry. He is sentenced to eight months imprisonment. In a confidential report written in relation to an appeal in another case made by Syme in May 1920, Chief Constables H. Morgan and J. Billings describe Syme thus: *'a man of morose and obstinate disposition, self-opinionated and of extreme views. He was always opposed to discipline and resented its application to himself or others. His attitude was that of a person who believed the whole fabric of the empire was saturated with wrongs that wanted setting right.'* In addition, they describe Syme as a *'misguided, self-deluded man who perhaps conscientiously believed he had a genuine grievance to ventilate and get put right.[8]'*

During the next ten years Syme continues to be arrested and imprisoned for his anti-establishment beliefs and public acts of civil disobedience, and is briefly committed to the Broadmoor Criminal Lunatic Asylum.

CHAPTER TWELVE

The Mother: Thursday 8th January 1914

Agnes Lineham's earliest memory is of being deserted by her Catholic mother at around the age of four, her birth not having been registered. Agnes in company with her two brothers John and Christopher, and her baby sister Mary, are found in the streets by a Parish Relieving Officer. They are taken to the Westminster Union Workhouse in the parish of St Anne in Soho on 13th September 1888[1]. Workhouses are in the charge of a Board of Guardians comprised of middle-aged, middle-class men with fixed ideas of the future lives of its occupants. Agnes is discharged from the Workhouse a week later and is sent to St Mary's Roman Catholic Girls' School, Walthamstow to be trained in the gender-specific practical skills of domestic service[2].

Agnes meets John Starchfield around 1898 and they marry on 12th October 1903 when she is approximately 20 years old[3]. For the sake of decorum, on the civil marriage certificate Agnes gives her address to the Registrar as that of next door to John in New Compton Street, St Giles. Her father is shown as deceased on the certificate. John states that his occupation is that of a Market Porter. Agnes falsely gives her occupation as a Preserve Maker, although she has been working as a Seamstress. In an over-subscribed working-class job market, many women who self-identify as Seamstresses are forced into the unsafe, twilight world of prostitution as opposed to the drudgery of precarious employment.

By 1914, the trade union for female jobbing workers like Agnes is entitled the National Federation of Women Workers. They campaign to expose 'sweated' labour, but she is not a member. Within the Women's Trade Union League, women Factory Inspectors conduct Court cases years before women are allowed into the legal profession. This is all for a minimum wage and for the protection of women workers from industrial accidents and diseases. Direct and forceful actions for women's rights by the Suffragettes has increased to the point where the government has invoked legislation known colloquially as the 'Cat and Mouse Act,' to curb the Suffragettes' hunger strikes[4]. However, Suffragettes are not generally single, poorly-paid, working women living in temporary accommodation with children to provide for.

During the next few years, Agnes and John's peripatetic lifestyle means that they endure the uncertainty of unfurnished tenancies in rundown properties within the inner London area. In late 1907 when they are living at 71 Commercial Road, Lambeth there is a fire at the property, a not unknown occurrence in those times, which forces them to move once again.

By 1909 Agnes is granted a separation order due to her husband's cruelty. She has given birth to two children in the intervening years, but both die before reaching school age. Each child has life insurance with the Pearl Assurance company at one penny a week. John and Agnes reconcile several times but by 1914 John has deserted her again. John's lack of maintenance is a constant headache for her as by now she is in sole charge of five-year-old Willie. John has better uses for the £1 a week that he is supposed to hand over to Agnes for child support, and this lack of regular financial support forces Agnes below the poverty line. Agnes is still a pretty woman at the age of thirty, but careworn from the double strain of being a single parent and the daily grind of looking for work. Her only employment option is in the poorly-paid, ready-to-wear tailoring job market of the East End. In 1914, Robert Tressell comments *"Poverty is not caused by men and women getting married...it's caused by Private Monopoly.[5]"*

On the fateful day of Willie's murder, Agnes leaves him in the charge of Emily Longstaff, her landlady. In her Police statement she relates how she returns home at 3pm, hearing the clock in the sitting room chime the hour as she enters the house. She calls out to Willie and Emily that she is back, but receives no response. She says that she has spent several hours in the company of a friend. She turns as she hears the front door open and sees Emily enter alone. On sighting Agnes, Emily cries out *"I have lost Willie!"* The colour drains from Agnes' face and she declares *"You are joking!"* Agnes recounts listening in disbelief and shock as Emily tells her how she sent Willie twice to the shop on an errand, Willie's failure to return from the second trip and Emily's fruitless search for him between Hampstead Road and Tottenham Court Road.

Agnes' Police statement continues with the account of how both women hastened to the nearby shop where the shopkeeper confirms Emily's account of Willie's appearance on an errand[7]. With growing anxiety, Agnes insists they extend their search to Camden Town. Having made numerous enquiries along the way with no success they return to Hampstead Road. Emily now suggests that they approach Willie's father and enlist his help in their search. Agnes quails at this saying that she has seen her husband in the street earlier that day and knows that if she tells John the boy is lost his reaction will be unpredictable. Deciding to attend the Police Station they are made aware that a boy's body has been found and are taken to the mortuary to ascertain if it is Willie. Agnes is too distraught to view the body. Consequently, Emily identifies the deceased boy as Willie, and Police enquiries begin.

CHAPTER THIRTEEN

The Curly-Haired Boy: Thursday 8th January 1914

Although it is a school day Willie does not expect to attend today. He has not attended school since before Christmas when he sustained a broken collar bone on Guy Fawkes' night having been knocked down by a car. He is taken to hospital. His arm is initially strapped then put into a sling. A statement provided to the Police by a Nurse Clayton on 18th March 1914 confirms that Willie attends the outpatients department of the hospital for massage on the 6th January 1914. In Nurse Clayton's opinion, he is nearly well but *"not strong enough to swing on gates or suchlike.*[1]*"*

The 1870 Education Act that is initially formed to ensure that all children attend school is ineffective due to parents relying upon income from their working children. Childhood is elusive for the children of impoverished parents as many are treated like mini-adults, with working responsibilities. In 1880, an amendment is enacted to assure that school attendance is compulsory for children aged between five and ten years, but is still not adhered to, especially for a child in Willie's impecunious circumstances.

Today, he is dressed in yesterday's clothes of trousers and shirt covered with a blue jersey with two misshapen buttons. Willie's mother, Agnes, does not allow his light brown hair to be cut, so it curls down to his shoulders. He does not trouble to check his appearance in the fragment of looking glass perched upon the fireplace mantle. If his mother makes enough money this week, and if she cares to, he may be taken to the public baths half a mile away off Warren Street to bathe and have his long, curly hair washed to stave off nits.

The weather is dull and mild with overcast skies with no ice forming on the inside of the only window in the room in which Willie and Agnes live. They inhabit a dingy, unfurnished, upstairs room in a lodging-house at 191 Hampstead Road. Fog will not roll in until that evening and will linger overnight. Willie and Agnes live a precarious existence, having done a 'moonlight flit' from their previous lodgings to avoid the cycle of 'tick' and rent day. Agnes permanently juggles whether to pay her meagre earnings for her rent or for her food 'debt' to the local grocer this week.

In 1898, Hampstead Road is described by Charles Booth, the social researcher and reformer, as being *"in a shocking state of repair."* Its social deterioration is still evident in 1914. Booth's perception of London is of a metropolis consisting of villages with little in common in the way of wealth and social status. He highlights areas by colour: light blue indicating those on the poverty line, dark blue areas contained the 'chronic' poor, and black streets of the semi-criminal[2].

Booth gives a human face to the myth of the underclass. One third of the East London population are living in poverty underpinned by poor wages. Booth's idea is to demolish the black streets and disperse those people into labour camps. His use of statistics is underpinned by Police files, Poor Law records and visits by the School Board. The Eugenics Society seeks to influence parenthood by preventing people with perceived 'undesirable characteristics' from procreating using a proposed programme of sterilisation. Booth's experiences contrast with the experiences of the novelist Henry James, who describes the streets of London as *"dreadfully delightful"* when he roams the streets of the capital carrying out his own social observations[3].

In the late 1800s, the poorest inhabitants are viewed through an atavistic lens of hereditary poverty as chattels. In Booth's time the practice of class tourism, known as 'slumming', is widespread. The upper-class fascination with the lives of the working-class poor manifests itself by paying money for tours, sometimes with guidebooks, of the poor housing conditions inhabited by the poor. There is a turning point in 1886 when after years of falling wages and terrible living conditions a demonstration of 13,000 working poor occurs in Trafalgar Square. They move from their geographical area of London and progress through the wealthy areas of the city. They are mocked by the well-to-do and retaliate by stoning the windows of the gentlemen's clubs; this becomes known as the West End Riots[4]. Eventually, a succession of strikes succeeds in obtaining better working conditions for 'sweated' workers like Agnes.

Today, Agnes is already up and doing in the kitchen having been out earlier seeking work as a Seamstress, with no avail. Willie no doubt hears her muffled conversation with Emily Longstaff, their landlady, as he runs down the stairs and into the kitchen. Agnes continually bemoans the fact that John, her estranged husband, and Willie's father, has not yet "divvied-up" her weekly maintenance, so she may only be able to pay a portion of the rent that week; a not unusual situation.

Agnes gives Willie a slice of bread pudding made with currants and raisins just out of the oven but he refuses it because his grossly decaying teeth give him toothache. His twenty 'milk' teeth need the services of a dentist, which is beyond his mother's pocket. His poor diet has affected the enamel on his teeth making them softer and prone to decay; the implementation of fluoride additives being decades away. As Willie does not attend school frequently enough, he cannot obtain the long-term benefit of free meals provided under the 1906 Education (Provision of Meals) Act. Willie begins his education at nearby Endell School, but leaves due to pneumonia. He attends St Andrew's School in Wall Street but this time catches scarlet fever. A short foray at All Soul's School in Foley Street ends with an infection of ringworm in July 1913 and he does not attend school since his accident.

Willie has few friends of his own age due to his non-attendance at school and is often cajoled into running errands for neighbours or Mrs Longstaff. His only friend at All Soul's School disappeared last year and the whisper was that he had been kidnapped to work the chimneys for a cruel Master. Willie expects to work in a factory when he gets older so that he can help his mother pay the rent. Between 1604 and 1914 Parliament enacts over 5,000 enclosure bills, estimated at around 6.8 million acres of land. This improves the agricultural productivity of farms but affects those agricultural labourers at the bottom end of the scale who rely upon their own parcel of land and tied cottage to exist. Many have consequently sought employment in the factories of the cities and have exchanged long working hours in the open air for long working hours within that fetid environment.

Agnes tells him to be a good boy and help Mrs Longstaff with her requirements as she herself is off to visit a friend in Soho Square and will be back this afternoon. As a bored Willie skulks in the backyard, he hears the 'clop-clop' of the milkman's horse's hooves in the road and smells the dung it deposits. The milkman shouts *'Milko.'* A thirsty Willie might consider asking Mrs Longstaff if he can take one of the blue and white jugs hung up on the kitchen dresser to fill up with milk. Unfortunately, on a previous occasion, he drops the jug and is severely scolded for his carelessness, so the milkman passes by the house unhindered.

On rare occasions, Willie is allowed to buy a muffin from the muffin man, choosing one from the tray he carries which is covered in a green baize cloth. In January 1914 such tradesmen are still plentiful in London, but soon their numbers will dwindle. There is a mad rush to sign up for voluntary enlistment in the surge of patriotism that sweeps the nation prior to the coming of war. By the end of the year, 300,000 of the men who sign up in 1914-15 appear to be under the Army's minimum age of nineteen, but many remain who have not come forward, leading to whispers of unpatriotic sympathies.

There is a widespread belief that shirkers are working-class with pastimes far removed from the 'hunting, shooting and fishing' of the upper classes. A popular rhyme posits:

"...Is it football still and the picture show,
The pub and the betting odds,
When your brothers stand to the tyrant's blow
And Britain's call is God's?[5]"

At a quarter to one, Mrs Longstaff calls Willie inside to carry out an errand. She normally requires a ha'penny loaf of bread from the shop up the road but this time gives Willie a note to give to the nearby Newsagent. Willie is to bring back two 'Unfurnished Apartment' cards so she may choose one for display in the Newsagents. On his way, Willie runs past the cat's meat dealer or carrier. The proprietor of the horse slaughterers' yard, from whom the carrier purchases the meat of dead horses, has a contract with brewers, coal merchants and the bus yards. The cooked and cooled flesh of the horses is weighed and the carrier buys it for re-sale to the public, ostensibly to be used for their pets.

The carrier cries "M-M-Meat" and sells horsemeat skewers from a tray slung in front of him. It is not unknown for the carrier to give credit to his customers and then bemoan the losses due to bad debt. Today, Willie carries no money for his dinner, let alone a meal of horsemeat for supper tonight. In the shop Willie plays with a toy on the counter while waiting for the Newsagent to fulfil Emily's request. The toy falls on the floor and Willie is scolded by the proprietor for his clumsiness, which makes him run back as quickly as he can with the cards for Mrs Longstaff. Mrs Longstaff chooses one to keep and tells Willie to return the unwanted one to the shop.

By now it is 1.30pm. Willie dawdles along Hampstead Road reluctant to return to the shop following his telling off. His route is a crowded thoroughfare with all kinds of people going for, or returning from, their dinner. Willie can smell freshly cut wood being fashioned into eggcups, bodkins, and candlesticks by the wood turner on his lathe. He hears a gypsy calling out *who will buy my sweet lavender?* But a small child goes unnoticed amongst the labourers, artisans of all callings, and housewives. Willie turns the corner and is swallowed up by the crowd, never reaching the shop and never returning home.

CHAPTER FOURTEEN

Aftermath

Unsolved murders are never closed; but passing decades impose their own statute of limitation. I first came across the Willie Starchfield murder when I was researching my dissertation for my Master's degree in Criminology and Criminal Justice. It resonated with me because Willie died on my mother's birthday. Initially, I skim-read through the case, unsurprised at 'just another' working class child death in the months prior to the beginnings of World War One in 1914. Newspapers initially named it as the 'North London murder', but that changed to the 'Starchfield Case', as events progressed.

1914 is a year of upheaval, and holds the beginnings of social change, although the class system continues to thrive. The British Empire allows the upper classes in Great Britain to benefit and prosper; although others, like Willie's parents, eke out a meagre existence with no prospect of advancement, and little hope. As I researched the case more thoroughly, I realised that Willie's tale does not end with his death. Indeed, the ramifications of the case impacted upon the daily lives of the main characters. The main protagonists continue with their lives, some more successfully than others.

William Gough:

Following the collapse of the trial, William Gough continues his career in the service of the Metropolitan Police. Gough's high profile and his association with Scotland Yard mean that he has connections with the Pinkerton Detective Agency in the USA. He is photographed in Hot Springs, Arkansas in 1920 with William A. Pinkerton and Len Houseman, who is described as a Newspaperman. In the photograph, Gough appears to be relaxed and confident in manner. He is formally attired in a well-pressed three-piece suit, a tie, and a starched shirt. A watchchain is attached to an inside pocket and a handkerchief is folded in his breast pocket. His shoes are highly polished. He wears a light-coloured 'pork pie' hat.

In 1927 Gough retires from the Metropolitan Police and pens a book entitled *'From Kew Observatory to Scotland Yard: Being Experiences and Travels in 28 Years of Crime Investigation'*. Gough's autobiography appeals to the 'general' reading public who are not satisfied with the mundane recitation of routine Police duties.

The revenue from this book financially assists Gough in his later years. His 4.5" x 7.5" personal calling card of the time reads: '(Residence:) | 8, Middleton Road, N.W.11 | Phone: Speedwell 2830. | William C. Gough, | Ex-Chief Inspector, | Criminal Investigation Dept. | New Scotland Yard. | 30, Duke Street, S.W.1. | Phone: Regent 4520.' Gough is one of several senior officers who publish their memoirs successfully.

The Victorian fascination with the occult, clairvoyance, séances, and mysteries extends into the 20th century. It is reflected in popular culture. There is a public 'taste' for accounts of real-life criminal cases in which the detective as 'hero' exhibits his honed skills in locating the perpetrator, 'righting wrongs' and thereby ensuring public safety. The detective, whether amateur or professional, as a distinctive occupation as a crime fighter became a distinct figure. In fiction, the private detective outshines his official counterparts á la Sherlock Holmes and Lord Peter Wimsey, whose mental prowess exceeds that of their Police detective peers who plod unimaginatively and stolidly towards a conclusion. These fictional super-detectives investigate the master criminals against whom they pit their wits. Their cases never include the mundane world of petty theft. Real-life criminal cases are modified and reproduced in theatres by actors, thrilling the crowds with their 'derring-do'.

The lower ranks of the Police are less inclined to publish their own stories as their occupational lives are more mundane. The Police reflect the class system; they emanate from working-class roots and struggle for social credibility. The fiction writer, Sir Arthur Conan Doyle, is contacted for advice on Willie's murder by the Police because he is considered an 'expert' on crime. He declines to assist them. One wonders if his response would have been different if Willie was not a 'working class' child.

In 1936 Gough travels to Australia with his wife by ship to visit his friend, the Chief of the Victorian State Police. En route to New Zealand, he arrests a jewel thief on board the ship, and hands him into Police custody on reaching Melbourne. The Victorian Police in Melbourne believe he is there to 'take over' as the new Police Chief, so view his visit with suspicion. There are public protests at this prospective 'Pommie' posting, which is widely reported in the local press. Gough denies these accusations but returns to London after a shortened visit, never to return. The Starchfield case remains his 'bête noir' in a glittering career at Scotland Yard.

Mr Bodkin for the Trial prosecution:

Bodkin is knighted in 1917 becoming Sir Archibald Henry Bodkin KCB. He dies on 31st December 1957 in Beechers Croft, Rogate, Sussex, England aged ninety-five years. One of the executors of his estate is Christmas Humphreys, described as a Barrister at Law. Bodkin's estate is valued at £124,385 6s 1d, a considerable amount of money at the time, but perhaps more modest than expected after a staunch law career. Bodkin's portrait hangs in the National Portrait Gallery in London and depicts him in profile wearing his wig and robes.

Mr Edward George Hemmerde for the Trial defence:

Hemmerde is born on 13th November 1871. He is a Barrister, Liberal and consequently, a Labour Member of Parliament. Hemmerde is first elected a Liberal MP at a by-election for East Denighshire in 1906. Hemmerde strongly supports Lloyd George's land enquiry. He is out of Parliament after 1918 and, in the early 1920s, along with most of the pre-war group of land-taxing Liberal MPs, joins the Labour Party. He has a final stint in Parliament as Labour MP for Crewe 1922-24. Outside Parliament Hemmerde is a Recorder of Liverpool from 1909 until his death. He is portrayed in several prints held at the National Portrait Gallery wearing his Barrister's wig.

Ex-Inspector John Syme:

Syme's wife endures years of personal and financial suffering and cold-shouldering by her local community. The tide turns too late for her and her husband's precarious situation in 1930, when a Home Office review of his circumstances offers him a lump sum of £1,200 plus a yearly allowance of £72, plus a government post. This is in respect of his claim for compensation for his dismissal in 1910. By 1931, a final settlement is agreed, and a statement confirming this made in the House of Commons. When interviewed by newspaper reporters, Syme maintains that he has spent three years in prison and six months in Broadmoor *"...for acts that were alleged to be wrong – the only way in which I could draw attention to my case..."* Syme suspends his actions against the authorities in 1940 and dies in hospital in 1945 leaving his widow and one son. The Government's failure to recognise falling Police pay and conditions is called to account by the Labour Party and the trade union movement. In due course, the Government capitulate to Police demands for a registered Police union.

Mrs Emily Longstaff, the landlady:

Emily fades into obscurity following the trial. The rest of her life will have been overshadowed by her guilt at sending Willie off on an errand from which he never returns.

John Starchfield, Willie's father:

There is a short hiatus in which John disappears following the collapse of the Trial for the murder of his son. On Saturday 11th April, he pens a statement for *John Bull*, in which he provides his own version of his life events and what he would have said in the Trial in his own defence. He reappears in April 1914 in Manchester, and is reported to star as the principal character in a film dealing with his life story. It is entitled *'Starchfield's Character Vindicated.'* That same year he also begins a tour of the country appearing in music hall theatres giving his version of his Army service, the Titus affair, and the Trial collapse to packed houses, for which he is handsomely paid.

Capitalising on his recent fame, he is approached by the Hewitt Film Producing Company to act in a film aptly entitled *'Was It He?'* There are many such film companies producing short films in the early 1900s. The film script describes the attempted kidnapping of a small boy. John acts the part of a Newsvendor who is wounded, and then becomes a Gardener eventually saving his employer's son from kidnap. The cast is small and consists of John, and Horatio Bottomley, as himself. The film no longer exists.

John dies in the St Pancras Infirmary in April 1916 as a result of the wounds he received when he was shot in the stomach by Titus. An odd circumstance occurs after his death, when a bottle is retrieved from the river Thames. It contains a hand-written paper which purports to be a confession by John that he killed his son; its veracity remains unproven.

Agnes Starchfield, Willie's mother: 23rd June 1914

Police Constable Munday's Police pocketbook records that last night he spies Agnes standing motionless in the middle of one of London's dingiest streets. The nearby church clock is striking three quarters past the midnight. There are tears streaming down her face and her lips move soundlessly in response to the anxious cries of the voices within her head. He notices that she has no hat and that her long hair is matted from days of neglect.

The fingers of her roughened right hand are wound tightly around the object in the pocket of the nightgown she wears under her thin coat. He is shocked to see that she is otherwise naked on this warm June night. She appears to have no shame at her state of near undress. He asks *"What is the matter with you?"* Agnes looks past him into the nothingness of the night. She is beyond everything now. She replies," I *want to go to the angels"* and, raising her right arm, looks upwards *"... and I am going there tonight."* She does not protest when

Munday takes her into custody to appear in Court in the morning.

Agnes stands in the dock of Marylebone Police Court. Munday reads out the charge that she has attempted to take her own life last night. The note found in her pocket indicating suicide is read out: *"Everyone is against me because I am married to him. It is impossible to live without my baby...He has left me to bear my trouble and sorrow and alone. Don't let him follow me."*

The Magistrate, having heard mitigation from Mr Boswell, a Missionary, views Agnes with a mix of pity and contempt. He remands her to the cells for one week for an offence against public propriety. She will be aware that suicide is a mortal sin in the Catholic faith. He looks to Agnes' older brother John who sits in the well of the court and advises him to take care of her on her release. There is no-one else to assist her, or anyone who possesses the ability to assess her mental state.

Following the inquest into her son's death, the details of the Coroner's investigations have become public knowledge; and within her working-class neighbourhood she has fallen foul of whisperings from neighbours. The unanswered questions of culpability emanating from the death of her son and subsequent trial follow her wherever she goes.

Approximately one month later, Agnes is again in the newspapers. On Tuesday July 28th 1914 Agnes is summonsed to appear at Marlborough Street Court before Mr Denman, the Magistrate, for assaulting Lucy Dalgarno, a married woman of Wells Street off Oxford Street.

Henry Margetts, prosecuting, (who was one of John Starchfield's Defence Barristers in the murder Trial) says that Mrs Dalgarno, the aggrieved, was interviewed by the Police in connection with that Trial. Mrs Dalgarno knew Agnes and was on friendly terms with her at the time her child was murdered.

Mrs Dalgarno's connection with the Trial causes ill-feeling between the two women and results in the assault taking place. The aggrieved states that on the night of July 18th 1914, Agnes, the defendant, came up to Dalgarno in Wardour Street and called her "A_twicer."

Dalgarno replied *"What did you call me that for? For screening you in your trouble?"*

The defendant does not answer, but instead strikes Dalgarno two blows on the nose with her fist.

On cross-examination Dalgarno says that if she had struck Agnes then it was in self-defence.

Agnes's evidence is that Dalgarno came up to her on that evening and said *"Here you are. What about my screening you from the Police?"*

Agnes replies *"What do you mean?"*

Whereupon Mrs Dalgarno strikes her: they then both 'close' falling to the ground. Agnes states that she merely acted in self-defence.

Mr Denman says that the defendant seems to be a neurotic and unstable sort of woman. Agnes is found guilty and bound over in the sum of £5 to keep the peace for 12 months; an extortionate sum at the time being the equivalent of fifteen days wages for a skilled craftsman. No leeway is given to Agnes considering the murder of her child six months previously; nor her previous court appearance on 23rd June 1914 when it would have been obvious that she was suffering from mental distress. No more is heard from Agnes until 1916.

On 13th January 1916, Agnes is registered at the Kentish Town number 1 branch of the National Union of Railwaymen as an Engine Carwasher. Photographs of women Carwashers at the time show that they wear leather overalls and clean the outside of the railway engines and carriages. Agnes resigns in June 1920 with other women. No superannuation is recorded in the register. It is likely that, as a women worker, she is not considered to be a permanent employee of the railway company, nor a permanent member of the Union, and consequently does not pay towards the Union's pension fund. The distinction drawn between male and female workers can be seen in the First World War registers – entries for the men are in standard black ink, women are recorded in red.

Agnes became a widow once John died in 1916 as a direct result of his wound. In April 1921 an Agnes T Sarchfield marries Frederick Town, a Printer, and they move to the Romford area. Agnes Starchfield previously records in a Police statement that her surname by marriage was 'Sarchfield' without the 'T.' My belief is that this is Agnes adding a middle name of Teresa to her second marriage certificate to remove herself from the notoriety of the murder case.

Sadly, Frederick Town commits suicide aged 49 years in December 1929 in a railway station waiting room after working a night shift. At Frederick's Inquest, Agnes Town confirms it was a happy marriage, and that they were making plans for Christmas. She cannot give any explanation for Frederick's suicide.

In July 1930, an Agnes T Town marries a William G. Wood, both of Romford, Essex.

In 1958 an Agnes T Wood dies in Thanet, Kent.

Horatio Bottomley, Newspaper Proprietor:

Bottomley is variously described as a journalist, author, newspaper publisher, financier, and maverick politician. He wears all those hats. Bottomley sets up the weekly tabloid *John Bull* which is dedicated to supporting the working man. Bottomley is a superb orator, and a strong opponent of Germany, holding rallies in Trafalgar Square, and using *John Bull* for his jingoistic commentary. He is a strong proponent of 'Englishness' and propounds:

"If by chance you should discover one day in a restaurant that you are being served by a German waiter, you will throw the soup in his foul face, if you find yourself sitting at the side of a German clerk, you will spill the inkpot over his vile head."

His connection with John begins when he hears about John's arrest. Bottomley pays for John's defence team under the auspices of John being a Newsvendor and a retired soldier. More copies of *John Bull* are sold to a public eager for salacious gossip, thus profiting Bottomley's pockets. After the Trial collapse, Bottomley's column castigates the Police for not following up other leads in the case. He eventually takes a small part in the film *'Was it he?'* He dies penniless in 1933.

W. Wynn Westcott, Coroner:

In 1907 Westcott writes a survey of his work so far. It is entitled *Twelve Years' Experiences of a London Coroner.* This work describes his intense dislike of undertakers and their practices. He touches upon how many of the poor of the district insure the lives of their children for small sums with organisations like the Prudential; these sums are enough to pay for their burial. This is precisely what Agnes does for her three children.

Westcott now expresses a very low opinion of Jurymen. In his opinion... *"only a small proportion ever ask questions, but occasionally one meets with an eccentric genius, or a cantankerous or unreasonable man to whom nothing seems right."* Westcott continues with his occult practices until his death in South Africa in 1925.

MY CONCLUSION

I believe that John Starchfield wilfully murders his son, Willie, on 8th January 1914. He has the means, the motive, and he grasps the opportunity. The murder is pre-meditated. John always carries a cord in his pocket, a cord that is used to tie up bundles of newspapers; he uses this to strangle Willie. John murders Willie because seven days before the murder, the money that he was awarded for his heroism in the Titus affair ends. John uses part of this money, on an intermittent basis, to support his estranged wife Agnes and their son. When the Carnegie Fund money ends, he realises that his income as a Newsvendor will only support himself.

Agnes is vociferous in her demands for financial support. She approaches various organisations for financial help when John fails to support her. John's Military Form attests that he has served two spells of three months hard labour because he had deserted Agnes and Willie.

John's time as a British soldier in the Second Boer War, in which he received his 'clasps' for military service, most probably left him with post-traumatic stress disorder (PTSD). The South African war zone in which he serves is brutal. The Boers carry out 'lightning' attacks on the British soldiers leaving them in a state of hypervigilance. On the day of the Titus incident, John is on his way to the public house when he is wounded. I believe that he mentally reverted to his experience in South Africa and tackled Titus using his soldier's automatic reflex when he hears gunfire.

James Starchfield, John's brother, who spells his name 'Sarchfield' without the letter 'T', is interviewed by a reporter from the *Daily Mirror* newspaper two days after the murder. In this published interview, James confirms that he and his brother were both soldiers in South Africa. He says that his brother is *"...as kind-hearted a fellow as you would find anywhere, and he was awfully fond of his little boy."* It is James's contention that Willie is murdered out of revenge by an Anarchist connected to the Titus affair.

The same article ponders on the actions of 'lunatics,' and whether one murdered Willie, which I rebut. The *Daily Mirror* obtains a 'soundbite' interview from a doctor who has made a special study of the criminal psychology of lunatics. He states in a banner sub-heading *"Far too many lunatics are at large."* The article continues with the broad assessment by the same doctor that *"They may be harmless enough at the moment of escape; but fear or hunger may subsequently bring them into a dangerous mental state."* One wonders how many of the witnesses or Jurymen at the Trial read this article. Indeed, Clara Wood when questioned at the Trial mentions that one of her impressions of the man with the child was that of a 'lunatic,' mentioning that *"his eyes looked fixed."*

On John's return from South Africa, I contend that he has a reliance upon alcohol, and lives a peripatetic lifestyle with or without Agnes; this is a part of his PTSD condition. Their two previous children die under five years of age, and the parents benefit from these deaths as both children's lives are insured with the Prudential Insurance Company.

The question of how John knew Willie would be out in the street on an errand is easily solved. It appears that Willie was routinely unsupervised as his school attendance is erratic. Too young for regular work, he is consistently sent out on errands by Emily Longstaff, neighbours, or Agnes, to the corner shop or elsewhere. John probably lingers in the area for several days running waiting for sight of his son. The Hostel Manager at the Trial admits that there are two staircases in the building, and that he cannot swear who is on site at any given time. Once John sees Willie, he seizes his opportunity. It would have been easy for John to apprehend him. Willie probably indicates that he does not want to return to the shop because he has been told off. He may have forgotten his errand in the excitement of a promised day out, possibly to the seaside, on a train. A five-year-old Willie willingly goes off with his seldom-seen father.

John was a risk-taker with a plan, and to keep Willie quiet he buys him a bun as a treat. This is confirmed by Mrs Wood's statement and her identification of John at both the Inquest and the Trial. Mr White remembers seeing them at the ticket office and confirms this at the Trial but did not see them board the train.

John buys only one ticket when he and Willie board the local train. John strangles Willie with the cord within minutes of entering the carriage. He does not fear being interrupted because he knows that no-one will hear Willie cry out. Each carriage is separate from each other, and there is no interconnecting corridor.

John is unaware that Willie was *status lympaticus,* and so Willie dies in under two minutes of strangulation, according to Dr Spilsbury's Trial evidence. John callously places Willie's small body under one of the seats, anticipating that it will not be found for some time. He leaves the train, disposing of the cord out of the carriage window. It falls onto the railway line where it is later discovered by the Police searching the tracks. It is later identified as the type of cord which is used to tie up bundles of newspapers.

Finally, John would have been hanged if he had been found guilty. I believe that he pays other men in the lodging house to give him an alibi; for example, Tilley, who gives evidence at the trial. Once the case collapses, John has no shame when recounting the events of the trial, and his lucky escape from death. He portrays himself in a good light to audiences in music halls up and down the country, who pay to hear his account. Perhaps he hopes that his appearance as a hero in the film *'Was it He?'* will clear his character and his conscience, and re-write history.

In conclusion, 'landmark' cases are regurgitated and re-investigated from time to time but Willie Starchfield's murder is not a landmark case because it has had no lasting effect on existing law. Willie's case is significant as it remains unsolved, the murder victim was a child, and it is reported widely and discussed avidly at the time. Neither is Willie's murder a 'signal' crime, being one which heightens public fear of crime whether through media reportage or direct experience. The circumstances of Willie Starchfield's murder can be construed as a moral panic: child murder; newspaper coverage; an inquest; an arrest; a trial; many hundreds of mourners attending the funeral; and the murder superseded the outbreak of war. Moral panics denote them as having five stages: a threat to common values; the threat recognized within the media; a rapid heightening of public concern around the event; a response from the authorities; and finally, the event receding from the public consciousness.

Lasting curiosities of the case:

1. The theme of railways runs through Agnes's life. Her son dies on the railway, she works on the railway in World War One, and, if I am correct about her further marriages, her second husband Frederick commits suicide in a railway waiting room.

2. The length of Willie's hair. I surmise that Agnes wanted a baby girl and therefore kept Willie's hair long. The fashion for boys at the time was short hair. The post mortem shows that Willie has male genitalia. This anomaly remains a mystery.

NOTES

Chapter 1: The Funeral

1. Meller, H., B. Parsons. 2021. *London cemeteries: an illustrated guide and gazetteer*. Cheltenham. The History Press.
2. Anon. 1914. Pathetic Scenes are Witnessed. *Dundee Courier.* 19 January. p6.

Chapter 2: The Crime Scene

1. London Transport Museum. Available from: https://www.ltmuseum.co.uk/collections/research/library
2. Op.cit.
3. Op.cit.
4. The British Newspaper Archive. 1914. Who killed Willie Starchfield? *The People.* 11 January. p8.
5. Op.cit.
6. Met Office Library & Archive. Available from: https://digital.nmla.metoffice.gov.uk/file/sdb%3AdigitalFile%7C93ccec3a-f8c1-48b8-a5b8-378fd0563fee/

Chapter 3: The Autopsy

1. The British Newspaper Archive. 1914. The Murdered Child. *Daily Herald.* 16 January. p6.
2. Burney, I., N. Pemberton. 2011. Bruised Witness; Bernard Spilsbury and the Performance of Early Twentieth-Century English Forensic Pathology. *Medical History.* 55. pp41-60.
3. Rose, A. 2007. *Lethal Witness: Sir Bernard Spilsbury Honorary Pathologist.* Kent. Ohio. The Kent State University Press.
4. Op.cit.
5. Sir Bernard Spilsbury's autopsy index card notes. Available from: https://wellcomecollection.org/works/fc4wazd2

Chapter 4: The Inquest

Day One:

1. SRIA. Province of Greater London. 2023. *William Wynn Westcott 1848-1925.* Available from: https://srialondon.org/william-wynn-wescott/
2. Gilbert, R. A. 1997. *Revelations of the Golden Dawn.* UK. W. Foulsham & Co. Ltd.
3. Anon. North London Train Mystery. *The Times (London, England).* Friday 16th January 1914. p. 46. Issue 40422.
4. Contemporaneous record viewed at the British National Archives 2018.

5. Anon. The North London Murder. *The Times (London, England).* Wednesday 14th January 1914. p.5. Issue 40420.
6. British National Archives. Metropolitan Police Notepads signed 'as seen' by Gough and viewed on site by author.
7. Islington Local History Centre, London. Records viewed on site by author.
8. Anon. Did you kill Emily Dimmock? Camden Town Murder Trial. Wood's Fight for Life. Ruby Young's Great Ordeal. Prisoner Leaves the Dock a Free Man. 1907. *Aberdeen People's Journal.* Saturday 21st December. Available from: https://www.britishnewspaperarchive.co.uk/viewer/bl/0000773/19071221/097/0006
9. British National Archives. Transcripts viewed on site by the author.
10. Ibid.

Day Two:

1. The Train Murder. Remarkable Evidence at the Inquest. Movements of the Boy's Father. *The Times (London, England).* Friday 23rd January 1914. p.7. Issue 40428.
2. Ibid.
3. Ibid.
4. Ibid.
5. Ibid.
6. Ibid.

Day Three:

1. Sensational Evidence at the Inquest. Starchfield Dramatically Singled Out. *Yorkshire Evening Post*. Thursday 29th January 1914.p.8. Available from: https://www.britishnewspaperarchive.co.uk/viewer/bl/0000273/19140129/201/0008
2. Ibid.
3. Ibid.
4. Ibid.
5. Contemporary document of this arrangement viewed on site at the British National Archives by the author.
6. Op.cit.
7. Op.cit.

Chapter 5: The Detective

1. Gough, W. 1936. A Detective is Born and Not Made. *Advocate,* Wednesday 18 November, p.9
2. Gough, W. 1927. *From Kew Observatory to Scotland Yard: Being Experiences and Travels in 28 Years of Crime Investigation*. London. Hurst & Blackett
3. Taylor, D. 1998. *Crime, Policing and Punishment in England, 1750-1914*. Basingstoke and London. Macmillan Press Ltd
4. The Word. 2021. *Forensic Fingerprinting Analysis and History*. Available from: https://detectives.theworduk.org/forensic-fingerprinting-analysis-and-history/

5. Nubiya, O. 2023. *Who were the African people living in Medieval and Tudor England?* Available from: https://www.bbc.co.uk/bitesize/articles/z8gpm39

6. Aliens Act. 1905. Available from: https://www.legislation.gov.uk/ukpga/1905/13/pdfs/ukpga_19050013_en.pdf

7. Peek, F. 1883. *Social Wreckage-A Review of the Laws of England as they affect the Poor.* p. 32. London. Wentworth Press (23 February 2019).

8. Census Records. 2023. The National Archives. Available from: https://www.nationalarchives.gov.uk/help-with-your-research/research-guides/census-records/

9. Archives. 1913. *The Express & Telegraph, Adelaide.* 12 July. p.6. Available from: https://trove.nla.gov.au/

Chapter 6: The Investigation

1. www.britishnewspaperarchive.co.uk. John Starchfield appeared in court on remand several times prior to the Trial. These appearances were widely and avidly reported by all the main London newspapers and cascaded to local newspapers all over Britain.

2. Ibid.

3. ibid.

4. Ibid.

Chapter 7: The Affidavit

1. Starchfield Case. London Editor ordered to pay £100. *Daily Citizen (Manchester)*. Wednesday 22th April 1914. Available from: https://www.britishnewspaperarchive.co.uk/viewer/bl/0002672/19140422/045/0002
2. The Starchfield Case: Application to Commit An Editor. *The Times* (London, England), Wednesday 4th March 1914. p. 3, issue 40462

Chapter 8: The Father

1. Bullman, J. N. Hegarty, and B. Hill. 2013. *Charles Booth. The Secret History of Our Streets. A story of London.* UK. BBC books.
2. Op.cit.
3. British Army Service Records. 1897. Available from: https://www.findmypast.co.uk/transcript?id=GBM/WO96/969/1498905
4. British Army Service Records. 1899. Available from: https://www.findmypast.co.uk/transcript?id=GBM/WO97/5985/1067404
5. Conversation with staff at the Rifles Museum, Peninsula Barracks, Romsey Road, Winchester, Hampshire
6. Ibid
7. Forces War Records. Ancestry. Available from: https://uk.forceswarrecords.com/image/589764136/starchfield-john-page-1-uk-royal-hospital-chelsea-pensioner-service-records-1760-1925.

8. Op.cit.
9. Anon. 1912. Titus at Bow Street. *Reynold's Newspaper.* Sunday 29 September. p3. Available from: https://www.britishnewspaperarchive.co.uk/viewer/bl/0000101/19120929/041/0003
10. Stephen Titus, Killing. November 1912. Available from: httpps://www.oldbaileyonline.org.jsp?div=t19121105-33
11. Donaldson, C. 2018. In a letter to the author confirming the details of the award and Starchfield's name on its Roll of Honour.

Chapter 9: The Trial (1)

1. Bottomley, H. Who is Starchfield? *John Bull.* Saturday 21st February 1914. Available from: https://www.britishnewspaperarchive.co.uk/viewer/BL/0003234/19140221/030/0008?browse=False
2. Anon. Starchfield on Trial in Connection with Son's Death. Prisoner's Hair is Turning Grey. Landlady and the Boy's Disappearance. *Dundee Evening Telegraph.* Tuesday 31st March 1914. p.3. Available from: https://www.britishnewspaperarchive.co.uk/viewer/BL/0000563/19140331/063/0003?browse=False
3. Grant, T. 2019. *Court No. 1 The Old Bailey. The Trials and Scandals that Shocked Modern Britain.* Great Britain. John Murray Publishing.

4. Anon. The Sack Murder. *Kentish Express.* Saturday 7th February 1914. Available from: https://www.britishnewspaperarchive.co.uk/viewer/bl/0003535/19140207/098/0007
5. Op.cit.
6. Contemporaneous statement by Police Constable Attersoll dated 19th March 1914. Viewed by the author at the British National Archives.
7. Op. cit.
8. Op. cit.

Chapter 10: The Trial (2)

1. Contemporary transcripts of the Trial viewed on site at the British National Archives by the author.
2. Anon. Trial Breakdown. A Dramatic Scene. Judge Condemns Coroner. *Hampshire Telegraph.* Friday 3rd April 1914. Available from: https://www.britishnewspaperarchive.co.uk/viewer/BL/0001973/19140403/252/0013?browse=False
3. Ibid.
4. Ibid.

Chapter 11: The Revolutionist

1. Hansard. 1911. *Inspector Syme (Metropolitan Police).* Debated Wednesday 15 March. Available from:

https://hansard.parliament.uk/commons/1911-03-15/debates/91390784-2de7-4f06-851c-50f307af3efb/InspectorSyme(MetropolitanPolice)

2. Liverpool City Police. *Police Strike 1919.* Available from:https://www.liverpoolcitypolice.co.uk/articles/police-strike-1919/

3. Archive, Communist Party of Great Britain. 2023. *Miscellaneous Syme-related documents.* Available from: https://communistpartyarchive.org.uk/group.php?cat=&sid=&cid=CP-IND-MISC&date_option=equal&page=&pid=CP-IND-MISC-16

4. Parliament UK. 2023. *1913 Cat and Mouse Act.* https://www.parliament.uk/about/living-heritage/transformingsociety/electionsvoting/womenvote/case-study-the-right-to-vote/the-right-to-vote/winson-green-forcefeeding/cat-and-mouse-act/

5. Woodman, C. 2018. Spycops in context: A brief history of political policing in Britain. *The emergence of British intelligence: a product of the imperial boomerang effect.* p10. Available from: https://www.crimeandjustice.org.uk/sites/crimeandjustice.org.uk/files/Spycops%20in%20context%20%E2%80%93%20a%20brief%20history%20of%20political%20policing%20in%20Britain_0.pdf

6. The National Archives. MEPO318/18. Available from:https://discovery.nationalarchives.gov.uk/details/r/C1257860
7. The National Archives. MEPO3/1832. Available from: https://discovery.nationalarchives.gov.uk/
8. Miller, I. 2016. *A History of Force-Feeding. Hunger Strikes, Prisons, and Medical Ethics, 1909-1974.* p. 179.UK. Palgrave MacMillan.

Chapter 12: The Mother

1. London, England, Workhouse Admission and Discharge Records, 1764-1921. Available from: https://www.ancestry.co.uk/discoveryui-content/view/4019970:60391?tid=&pid=&queryId=ee71ef4daf4a6104cf8d44a6459be864&_phsrc=FLp37&_phstart=successSource
2. London, England, Workhouse Admission and Discharge Records, 1764-1921. Available from: https://www.ancestry.co.uk/discoveryui-content/view/4020019:60391?tid=&pid=&queryId=ee71ef4daf4a6104cf8d44a6459be864&_phsrc=FLp38&_phstart=successSource
3. England and Wales, Civil Registration Marriage Index, 1837-1915. Available from: https://www.ancestry.co.uk/discoveryui-content/view/17904472:8913?tid=&pid=&queryId=ebdb7072683c58910cc27262f03c131a&_phsrc=FLp42&_phstart=successSource

4. Miller, I. 2016. *A History of Force-Feeding. Hunger Strikes, Prisons, and Medical Ethics, 1909-1974.* p.179. UK. Palgrave MacMillan.
5. Tressell, R. 1914. *The Ragged Trousered Philanthropists.* London.

Chapter 13: The Curly-Haired Boy

1. Metropolitan Police: Office of the Commissioner: Correspondence and Papers. MEPO 3/237B. Available from: https://discovery.nationalarchives.gov.uk/resul ts/r?_q=starchfield
2. London School of Economics and Political Science. 2016. *Charles Booth's London.* Available from: https://booth.lse.ac.uk/
3. James, H. 1888. The city of dreadful delight. 13 December. *Pall Mall Budget.* Available from: https://www.printsandephemera.com/ourshop /prod_6849412-The-City-of-Dreadful-Delight-London-as-described-by-Mr-Henry-James-1888.html
4. Brodie, M. 2013. Artisans and Dossers: The 1886 West End Riots and the East End Casual Poor. *The London Journal.* Available from: https://www.tandfonline.com/doi/abs/10.1179 /ldn.1999.24.2.34
5. Begbie, E. H. Poster. *Your Country Needs You – Fall In.* Available from: https://www.iwm.org.uk/collections/search?fil ters%5BagentString%5D%5BBegbie%2C%20Ed ward%20Harold%5D=on

ACKNOWLEDGEMENTS

This book is dedicated to my daughter, Grace.

I am grateful to so many people who patiently assisted me with my enquiries when I was researching this book.

Dr Mike Darby, BDS, Southampton, for his information about Willie's teeth

Caroline Donaldson, Hero Fund Manager, Carnegie Hero Fund Trust, Fife

Liz Wood, Assistant Archivist, Modern Records Centre, University of Warwick

Oonagh Kelly, Walthamstow School, London

Caroline Warhurst, Library & Information Services Manager, London Transport Museum

'Catherine,' the Met Office Library & Archive, London

The staff of the Royal Green Jackets Museum, Winchester

The staff of the State Library of Victoria, Melbourne, Australia

The staff of the National Archives, UK

The staff of the Archives of the Communist Party

The staff of the Imperial War Museum, London

The staff of the Islington Local History Centre, London

The staff of the Wellcome Collection, UK

On a personal note, thank you to:

Nigel Brearley, my eminent PhD supervisor; Sue Hartley, who knows her 'Ps' from her 'Qs'; Genevieve Groom, who told me to just shut up and write the book; Candy Ofosu-Apeasah, author, and my dear university friend; Rhonda and Peter Prestidge, who listened; Kerrie McInnes, who enlightened me about the 'hoons'; Tony Carr, who helped me with his personal knowledge of London; Sarina Langer, the author, who got me back on track, and Becky from Platform House Publishing.

Susan is a Crime Historian and globetrotter,
with a background in law and psychiatry.

Printed in Great Britain
by Amazon

36233039R00088